MYSTERIES IN THE MIST

MIST, FOG, AND CLOUDS IN THE PARANORMAL

W.T. WATSON

BEYOND THE FRAY
Publishing

Published by Beyond The Fray Publishing

ISBN 13: 978-1-954528-25-3

Cover design: Disgruntled Dystopian Publications

Beyond The Fray Publishing, a division of Beyond The Fray, LLC, San Diego, CA
www.beyondthefraypublishing.com

BEYOND THE FRAY
Publishing

CONTENTS

INTRODUCTION

I know the strange names by which fogs and mists are woven and unwoven ...
Robin Artisson
Letters from the Devil's Forest

When I was doing the research for my first book, *Phantom Black Dogs: Walkers of the Liminal Way*, I sometimes encountered my subject emerging from mist or fog to astonish or terrorize the witnesses who recounted their stories. As I drilled down into more and more stories and widened my search for Black Dog stories, I, of course, had to search through the work of Linda Godfrey, Manwolf expert extraordinaire and extensive purveyor of all things canid and cryptid.

In the course of those searches, I came across another anomaly that caught my eye, the mention of a grey mist in relation to a Manwolf that Ms. Godfrey was trying to track in her native Wisconsin. In her wonderful book *Monsters Among Us*,

Godfrey details the "Smith" case where that mist was documented. Godfrey used a cover name to protect the witness.

"Smith" was a farmer who had a mystery on his hands. Something on his land was removing animal carcasses that he had set out as bait for his trail cams but was not being photographed. In one instance, the trail cam, focused on a deer carcass, took a picture in the night. The deer showed up intact at 10:17 p.m. The camera clicked at 10:42 p.m., but the picture showed that the carcass was completely covered by a "thick, rounded gray mist". For over six hours, the mist was there as the trail cam took over 100 photos of it. When the obscuration finally cleared, the deer carcass was missing, and the trail cam took perfectly normal pictures of the area.

In a separate incident, Smith's trail cams took many photos of a "soft, orangey mist" that formed into a rough oval in the branches of a nearby tree. Multiple cameras taking photos from more than one angle ruled out the explanation of lens flare or sun glare from the trail cams. Even more interesting, one of the cameras showed that the "mist's top edge was a much denser, orange oval that brightened and enlarged as the minutes passed, gradually forming a bright yellow, roughly circular center with deep orange 'wings' to either side ..."

This "artifact" in the photos reminded Godfrey (and me) of the orange anomaly sighted at Skinwalker Ranch that seemed to be a portal through which strange things moved back and forth, including UFOs and Sasquatch-like creatures.

Another "artifact" appeared in trail cam photos taken in the early summer. Smith had laid out a small road-killed deer and positioned a camera to take pictures every thirty-seconds in the daytime and then move to motion and heat detection at night. The following day there was a darkened but still visible shot followed, thirty-seconds later, by a photo in which the right half of the screen was completely obscured by an ink-black mist. The camera ultimately shot fifty-five pics of the mist before the anomaly disappeared.

The deer remained in place this time, but when Smith went to retrieve the SD memory card from the camera the next day, he noted that, "something had picked up the deer carcass and jammed its head and upper torso through the base of two small trees growing about eight feet away. The entire quarter of the animal's right front leg was separated almost surgically in a neat circle around the shoulder, and the whole leg was removed from the scene.

This mysterious visitor, when it left any trace behind, made four-plus-inch canine tracks and appeared to be bipedal, judging from its trail. When Smith and another farmer endeavoured to track the animal, they encountered and photographed yet another anomalous mist.

I now had mention of mists and fogs attached to both Phantom Black Dogs and Manwolves, and I found myself wondering if these mysterious environmental shrouds might be an ongoing theme in the realm of high strangeness. Once *Phantom Black Dogs: Walkers of the Liminal Way* was complete and off to the publisher, I endeavoured to find out.

My interest was not strictly academic. I also had a personal connection to strange mists. As a young man, I had a friend whom I will call Nate who suffered a terrifying encounter with mist.

Nate was one of the original "goth" kids – dressed in black, black fingernail paint and even, for the shock value, black eyeliner when he went out to clubs – and he loved role-playing games and dabbling in the darker side of the occult. Although I knew for a fact that Nate was not averse to hallucinogens, he swore to me that he was sober when this incident occurred, and I had no reason to doubt him. He had related tales to me before, and he was always careful to delineate between events that happened when he was high on an illicit substance or otherwise.

Nate was a night owl long before he affected the Goth look, but he had retired early since he had to work the next day. He woke in the night to use the restroom, and as he blundered into the hallway of his tiny apartment, still half asleep, he had to pass a large, oval mirror.

As he walked past, Nate looked into the mirror and was frightened to see that the surface of the mirror was clouded with "smoke". The smoke was frightening enough, but as he stood there, Nate felt that he was being pulled into the mirror. Later, he would acknowledge that it was his astral or etheric body experiencing this pull, but at the time, he felt that he was being pulled bodily into the reflective surface.

Fortunately for Nate, his girlfriend was sleeping over that night, and something awakened her. She found her boyfriend with his face firmly pressed against the mirror and, assuming that he was sleepwalking, pushed and shoved him away from the mirror. He "woke up" once the contact with the mirror was broken and returned to bed after some wild-eyed rambling. His girlfriend got the story from him in the morning when he was fully awake and cogent.

Now, I can't be absolutely positive that Nate's story was objective fact, but I can say that he experienced behaviour changes after the incident. That mirror stayed covered from then on, and he got rid of some questionable magical materials that he had around the house.

The combination of the strange stories in Linda Godfrey's work, my own research into Phantom Black Dogs, and that account from my own life was simply more than I could ignore, and I began the research for this volume shortly after completing *Phantom Black Dogs: Walkers of the Liminal Way.* I had no idea how deep this rabbit hole would go, but as the reader might surmise from looking at the table of contents, I found fogs and mists in the areas of cryptozoology, the paranormal and high strangeness.

In my research for this book, I have walked through the pages of academic articles as well as books by paranormal authors you will recognize and, perhaps, some that you will not. The source material stretches all the way from my own Black Dog book published in 2021 to tomes published in the 1600s.

I have discovered fog and mist stories in the unlikeliest places, starting with my own work with Phantom Black Dogs and reaching to Sasquatch tales and Linda Godfrey's assorted texts on the Manwolf phenomenon as well as academic and legendary work on vampires. The faery and ghosts appear as well as unidentified flying objects and the abductions that seem related to those UFOs in some way.

Most interesting of all, I have located a whole host of stories about mysterious mists with various effects on humans in addition to stories of mists associated with human teleportation and time slips. The puzzle of people who vanish without a trace is addressed in this book, and you might even find some clues to what actually happened to planes and ships in places like the Bermuda Triangle.

The book is divided into several sections for those who want to slip over to their favourite phenomena first. Section 1 will cover cryptid stories; Section 2 will address Otherworld beings, what some might call spirits; Section 3 will talk about UFOs and abductions. We will move on from there to Section 4, which deals with mysterious mists, time slips, teleportation, and disappearances. The final section of the book will deal with those encounters that did not fit well into the other sections but, I felt, deserved a place in the book; then I will conclude with some thoughts about just what the heck we are dealing with in these accounts.

A quick note before I begin. You will see me use the word paranormal throughout the book. I use the word in its widest connotation as indicative of phenomena that are beyond the scope of normal scientific understanding. I have adapted this usage to cast the widest net, and by its use, I am denoting the subjects of cryptozoology, the study of spirits and ghosts (with an occasional turn into psychic phenomena), ufology, and the bizarre Fortean stories about mist that will appear at the end of the book.

Let's begin our journey now where I left off in my last book, with the enigma of the Phantom Black Dog.

SECTION ONE

CRYPTIDS IN THE MIST

PHANTOM BLACK DOGS

As I noted in the introduction, this whole journey began as I was doing research for my first book on Phantom Black Dogs. The Black Dog is a more or less solid apparition that manifests itself most frequently along roads and other paths of human travel. The being most often appears as a very large black dog – sometimes described as the size of a calf or compared to a mastiff or Newfoundland dog – and in many of its permutations it is seen to have glowing, self-illuminated eyes.

The Black Dog most often differentiates itself from regular beasts by appearing and disappearing at will, but as I point out in the referenced text, a whole host of other phenomena are associated with sightings of this entity. The Black Dog is most often recognized as a death portent, but it also appears as a traveller's guardian in many of the old tales as well as demonstrating interesting abilities such as being able to change its size and being impervious to gunfire.

As I was putting together my notes for the Black Dog book, I noticed, time and again, that the weather for Black Dog sightings fell into three broad categories. Seen most often at dusk or in the night, the apparition appeared most often, in the tales I found, on clear days. Other tales swing to the opposite extreme, and the Black Dog is encountered on stormy, overcast days. Finally, there were several stories in my text in which fog or mist played an important role.

In the first of these encounters, the Black Dog plays its guardian role. In 1875, James Murray, the first editor of the Oxford English Dictionary, was with his children on a mountainside in Cumbria, UK, when they were all caught in a thick mist. A Black Dog abruptly appeared and refused to let them pass – a behaviour seen repeatedly with this apparition – until the mist cleared. When the family were able to see where they were going, they discovered that the Black Dog, which had vanished with the fog, had prevented them from walking off a steep precipice.

Another guardian Black Dog appears in a tale from Somerset, UK, where a cottager had climbed a hill in the Quantocks and had suddenly been socked in by the sea mist. The gentleman was afraid that he might freeze before he could find his way home. He was feeling his way along, growing increasingly distressed, when he touched shaggy fur. The man assumed he had his hand on his sheep dog and that the dog had come out to find him, so he directed the good boy to take him home.

Imagine this fellow's surprise when the dog guided him to the door of his cottage, and he heard his own dog barking inside. He turned to look at the animal that accompanied him and found that it was a Black Dog, which, as he watched, gradually grew larger and then faded from view.

Stories of the Black Dog would not be complete without at least one tale where someone shoots at our erstwhile apparition.

A fisherman named Sam Rudd had a run-in with a Black Dog on the beach at Salthouse, Norfolk, UK, that he would rather forget. As with our other stories, the tale begins with "an impenetrable mist" settling over the beach. Concomitant with the dense fog, Rudd began to hear the baying and howling of a dog in the distance. Norfolk is well known for its version of the Black Dog, called Black Shuck, which has a questionable reputation, so Rudd ran for his home and locked the doors up tight behind him.

Rudd's father seemed to be made of sterner stuff. The older man took his fowling gun, a shotgun designed for hunting birds, and went up to the second floor of the house. Throwing open a window, the father confirmed that there was, indeed, a Black Dog sitting in the yard, howling. Rudd's father unloaded on the Dog with no effect. When the two men investigated the next day, the only sign of the gunfire was their newly ventilated outhouse.

In a more modern story, we come to the tale of the so-called Hell Hounds of Meridean Island. This one has been investigated by such well-known writers as Chad Lewis and Linda Godfrey since it takes place in the state of Wisconsin. For my book, I pulled witness testimony from the television show *Monsters and Mysteries*, which featured two sets of witnesses – a couple having some time away from the kids, and a pair of paranormal investigators who wanted to check the story out – who had a similar experience.

Both sets of witnesses reported that their experience was preceded by a dense, cold fog settling in suddenly and without seeming cause, followed almost immediately by the feeling that something was wrong. The fog and agitated feeling were followed by growls coming out of the fog, which caused the witnesses to decide that it was time to vacate the area.

The two investigators claim to have seen the apparition of a woman who drowned in the area as well as a ragged-looking Black Dog with glowing red eyes. In both cases, the growling of the Black Dog chased the witnesses until they came to the road, where the pursuit abruptly broke off. This behaviour is common with Black Dogs, as the apparition often seems to have a defined territory beyond which it does not pass.

Before we leave the Black Dog realm and move on to other beings, a final story came to me by way of Peter McCue's *Britain's Paranormal Forests: Encounters in the Woods.* McCue cites an article by Nick Redfern that does not appear to be extant any longer in which a witness describes a frightening encounter with a Black Dog.

The witness was walking around Castle Ring, in the Cannock Chase area of the UK, in December of 1991 when he noticed:

> ... a small area of dense fog and went towards it. When he got within about 20 feet of it, he felt his hair become 'static and electrified', and he experienced an intense smell of burning metal. A monstrous black dog – about the size of a young horse – loomed out of the fog. The man and the dog slowly backed away from each other, with the latter retreating into the fog. When the man was maybe 150 feet from the fog, he saw a small ball of light zoom in over it and cast down a column of vivid blue light towards it. In an instant, normality was restored – the fog, the ball of light and the dog were all gone.

This business of static electricity in the air and strange smells, along with the ball of light in the fog, is something we will see over and over in the course of this book. I am simply going to make a note of it here, and we will comment more extensively later in the book, when we have more incidents logged.

In the meantime, as I mentioned in the introduction, the Phantom Black Dog is not the only creature that we can find in the mist.

MANWOLVES

Moving from Phantom Black Dogs to another dog-shaped anomaly, I cited one of Linda Godfrey's cases in the introduction, a weird one in which mist anomalies and a "visitor" that left canine prints that puzzled both Godfrey and the farmer on whose land the visitations occurred. While this case was up there on the high strangeness scale, I also noted that Ms. Godfrey's favourite subject, cryptid canids, seemed to appear from the fog on several occasions.

Before we move to some of those stories, however, let's take a look at another account that Godfrey relates in *Monsters Among Us* with another trail cam "artifact".

The initial incident took place on 17 July 2014 at a property outside Hartland, Wisconsin. The witness, whom Godfrey calls Susan, reported she was wakened by the barking of her small dog. Thinking the canine needed to go out, she took the animal out on the back deck, expecting it to "run out into the yard as was its habit". Instead, the small dog became silent and hid behind its owner.

Susan noted a tall, furry figure moving along the tree line at the back of the home. At first, the witness thought she was seeing someone in a "thick, gray jacket", but she soon realized that the figure was not human, and it wasn't wearing a jacket:

> Susan was stunned to see that its body was entirely gray-furred, although the fur appeared thickest on the creature's muscular chest to give it that jacket-like impression. Its head was that of an animal, with short, pointed ears on top of the head and a "short snout" like that of a boxer or other short-snouted canine, but "definitely not flat like a human's," she said. Its forelimbs hung at its sides and seemed muscular at the top, but they ended in longish paws with noticeable claws. They weren't long like a Bigfoot's, Susan noted, adding that its thighs were also muscular but thinned toward the lower limbs, and that it walked on its toe pads rather than flat-footed. "The legs were canine," she said. Measurements of a tree branch that the creature just barely passed beneath showed the animal stood about six feet tall.
>
> The Manwolf turned and looked at the witness and then walked off in the characteristic "I don't care if you see me" attitude of these creatures. Godfrey found tracks and other evidence to confirm the sighting.

Susan had further encounters on her property. What was particularly frightening for the witness was that the Manwolf seemed to have a particular interest in her special-needs child. Trail cams were deployed, and as with the Smith case, on 2 September, the cam showed footage of a "strange column of thick, translucent mist on the right side of the photo". Godfrey notes that two photos were taken and that in both photos a denser form seemed visible in the centre of the mist that looked "vaguely animal and vaguely human at the same time".

Now this story certainly makes it appear that the creature in question was using the fog/mist to obscure its presence as it came into our world. I will have much more to say about this in the conclusion to the book.

Sometimes, fog is simply fog though. Knowing this doesn't help when you have a very up close and personal run-in with a Manwolf.

The account is second-hand, presumably since the witness did not want to come forward, but Kevin, the teller of this tale from *Monsters Among Us*, states unequivocally that the witness has "matter-of-factly [stood] by her story. Even at the teasing of her [family]". Kevin also noted that the witness comes from a "strait-laced" family full of accountants, HR directors, teachers, etc., so one suspects that she did endure a good amount of flak about this story.

Our tale teller states that the woman came into the office in 1990, spluttering that is "wasn't a [expletive] man … and it wasn't a [expletive] dog!" The woman then related her story.

She had been headed home from a late shift, driving carefully through fog. The woman stopped at a four-way stop, and abruptly, "something" bounded onto the hood of her car. She got a good look at the thing on her hood and was so frightened that she stomped on the gas, forcing the creature to leap from the front of her vehicle. The "something" was grey in colour and had the head of a dog or wolf but with hands visible to her through the windscreen.

Once the creature had cleared her automobile, the witness drove away quickly and never drove that route home again. When Kevin helpfully pointed the woman to Linda Godfrey's website and specifically to some of Ms. Godfrey's illustrations, the woman turned "white as a sheet" and confirmed that the creature she saw looked like the website drawings.

Those who pose as skeptics but are only trying to maintain their materialist world view would point out that this encounter was brief. They might say that the witness had some perfectly natural animal jump on her car. Perhaps she mistook an errant bear or coyote for a Manwolf. Perhaps the admittedly foggy conditions hindered her perception, making her believe she was seeing something that she was not.

It's possible. High-stress situations can certainly cause misperception of events, but I would ask the doubters a couple of questions.

How often have you ever heard of a wild animal, such as a bear or a coyote, hopping unexpectedly onto the hood of a moving vehicle? Certainly, animals are struck by moving cars and trucks all the time, but the witness noted that the creature landed on her hood "with quite a bit of force and did so just as she was coming to a complete stop". That sounds to me like this being deliberately leapt on this vehicle, and that is not behaviour one commonly sees in wild animals.

Also, there is the matter of the hands. Bears, coyotes, wolves, etc. do not have hands, and the witness makes a point of stating that the creature had hands but the head of a dog or wolf. I find it doubtful that a person would mistake a paw, no matter how large, for a hand.

Our so-called skeptic might pull out the hoax defence at this point. I admit that it is possible that this could have been a human with a mask on, but the question then arises: why? If one wanted to scare the heck out of someone, why wait until late at night, when the pickings are thin? Why actually jump on the hood of the car when approaching the side of the vehicle from the fog would be every bit as scary? Given the visual limitation that such masks cause, the prankster would have had to be a real athlete to pull this stunt off and get away without falling and with the mask still in place.

I am not going to spend a lot of time looking at things from the so-called skeptic's point of view, but I thought that we might walk through the exercise early on to make a point. Sometimes a sighting might be explainable in materialist terms, but what we are looking at, in the paranormal and Fortean, is not a single incident. We are looking at the weight of evidence, all the hundreds or thousands of people who have had these high strangeness experiences. There really is no arguing with that mass of evidence if one has an even halfway open mind. Those who do continue to argue closed their minds long ago.

Now that we have that settled, on to more witnesses.

Monsters Among Us had another fog-wrapped Manwolf for our reading pleasure. This account occurs in 1991. The woman and her female companion were driving through North Carolina on their way to a vacation in Florida when they were forced to detour onto a "foggy, two-lane country road". In the spirit of a road trip, the two had the radio on and were chatting as they made their way along.

> Abruptly, "this large gray furry critter with glowing green eyes and eyeteeth showing ran across the road on its hind legs. I suspect," the witness said, "[that] the glowing came from our headlights reflected, like hunters jacking deer, but it was creepy."

When one sees an upright bipedal canid running across the road, one is forgiven for using the W-word – werewolf. The witness felt that the being "somehow looked like a cross between a dog or wolf and a human but not really describable".

At a range of about forty yards, the witnesses estimated the creature's height at seven feet, and they noted that it "looked wolfish about the head" but that the body did not really look human but more like a wolf had simply decided to locomote on its back legs.

Not surprisingly, the two witnesses got out of the area with all speed, got back to the highway, and drove straight through to Florida after stopping quickly at a truck stop.

Again, we see a Manwolf appearing from the mist and then disappearing just as quickly. The many stories of the Manwolf seem to indicate a high level of intelligence in these creatures. Perhaps they use the fog as cover during the hunt or other, unknown activities?

Lyle Blackburn, in his book *Sinister Swamps*, gives us another story from a reliable source trained to observe and keep a cool head under strain. This account happened in the Bridgewater Triangle area, in the Hockomock Swamp, in October of 2016. Hockomock is a First Nations word that means something along the line of the "place of the spirits".

The witness was a correctional officer named Hadley who was returning home from a shift, using the calm of the country drive to relax his nerves after spending time supervising convicts. The night had turned foggy, so the officer was proceeding carefully, but the witness states that visibility was still good.

As Hadley navigated a curve and turned his attention ahead:

> ... something darted from the swamp on the right and bounded across the road in full view of his headlights. It was a huge, dog-like creature running in a hunched-over fashion with its head low. Hadley instinctively tapped his brakes as the thing ran into the trees on the opposite side of the road, disappearing into the blackness.

The encounter was brief, but enough for the officer to get a good look at the beast. Though it was dog-like, he was sure it was not a dog. Nor was it a coyote or even a wolf. This thing was much larger and unusual with dark fur and a body like a hyena. On all fours it was as tall as the hood of his Nissan Altima, and if it had been standing, it was probably seven feet in height. It moved both like a canid and an ape and was altogether unlike anything he'd ever seen ...

Hadley estimated that his mystery beast passed no more than ten feet in front of his car. Covered in "long gray fur like a dog" with "dark, black skin on its underbelly", Hadley noted that the beast had its head down as though it was tracking something, and he even picked out a tail, although he could not tell if the tail was very short or tucked between its legs.

Notably, this man, who worked in prisons and was not easily intimidated, experienced a fight-or-flight response to the beast. "Something in my body was telling me to go ..."

Although he did not see the beast on two legs, I found it telling that he estimated the thing's height while standing up, as though he expected the creature, whatever it was, to pop up and begin bipedal locomotion at any moment. The barrel-chested, hyena-like creature reminds me of descriptions given by some peasants of the Beast of Gévaudan.

The fog in the above case was not visually limiting, according to the witness, but in another large cryptid canid sighting in March 2007, we find a witness stating that it was an "exceptionally foggy night". This sighting occurred in the north-east corner of Wisconsin and comes to us from the book *I Know What I Saw*.

The witness, reporting to Linda Godfrey, stated that there were three people in the car driving from Sheboygan to Madison, and visibility on the highway was "very poor". The witness was driving, and the other passengers were asleep as he encountered a "giant, white animal-like figure standing in the road".

The driver locked up his brakes to avoid hitting the creature while the beast stood and looked at him, apparently unconcerned and unmoving. The monstrous white creature was "about the size of a bear but had a wolf-like head and ears". Both passengers awakened in time to see the creature and confirm the driver's report.

Interestingly, this event occurred in the same general area as another incident in which a large "bear-wolf" – as local hunters had dubbed these enormous wolf-like creatures – seemed to try to shove a car off the road. Godfrey notes that no wild animal willingly stands and waits while a car barrels toward it, and wonders if the "bear-wolf" was not deliberately trying to force the car off the road.

Canned humans for dinner? I am happy that this driver managed to avoid finding out.

We will encounter more cryptid canids appearing from the fog in the next chapter.

I am relying heavily on the work of Linda Godfrey for this section since she is the recognized expert in the area of cryptid canines of all sorts. Her seminal work in this area was 2003's, *Beast of Bray Road* from which our next story comes.

On another thickly foggy night, the witness, Brichta, was driving a friend back to the campground where he was staying after a wedding reception. Although Brichta's mother stated that he felt he had run over something, perhaps a mailbox, in the thick fog, Brichta's recollection, when he spoke to Godfrey, was of seeing an enormous hand reaching out for his vehicle from the fog.

The witness went on to say that,

> "It was large; it's [*sic*] lower chest and belly was at the top of the car. It was whitish-gray with black streaks in it, and it was hairy ..." Like a previous witness, this young man perceived the beast as lighter hued than most witnesses. The witness

> also stated that, "I didn't get any facial details, but the lower part of the body I can describe to a T. It had large legs. The feet ... were a little fuzzy ... The fingers were either pointed or had quite the nails on them. The arm was long and kind of odd-shaped ..."

The witness also noted a foul odour and pointed out where the pinstripes on his car were damaged, supposedly by the beast. He insisted that he knew what a bear looked like from spending time at his parents' cabin up north and this being was not a bear. Brichta was convinced enough of the weirdness of his sighting to report the event to law enforcement, a fact Godfrey confirmed.

While, once again, we have a creature appearing out of the fog, in this case, since the witness offers no description of the head at all, one must wonder if this young man encountered the Beast of Bray Road or a wandering Sasquatch that happened to be in the neighbourhood.

In her book *Werewolves,* Godfrey gives us the story of one of the original Beast of Bray Road witnesses. This story actually occurs on Halloween night 1991, Samhain to folk in the Neo-pagan community, a time when the Veil Between the Worlds is said to be thin.

Doris Gipson was on her way to retrieve a young relative from a party on that foggy evening just outside the town of Elkhorn, Wisconsin, and she chose to shortcut along the three-mile length of Bray Road. As with Brichta above, Gipson thought that she might have hit something, and fearing she had done in someone's dog, she stopped. Getting out of her car, the woman took a few steps in the direction of the perceived accident.

To her horror, as she was almost clear of her car, the woman saw "... a large creature emerge from the fog. It was running straight toward her on two legs". Gipson told Godfrey, "It was no dog; it was bigger than me ..."

The monster moving toward her on the road had a "powerful build, a head like a wolf or a dog, and was covered in shaggy fur." The beast was heavy enough to make sound as it charged her, and the witness leapt back into her car and took off. The beast left scratch marks on Gipson's car.

Gipson's story, along with others in the area, caused Godfrey to begin digging into the Bray Road incidents and inadvertently launched the author on a career of tracking canid cryptids.

I find it curious that we have so many of these stories of Manwolves, bear-wolves and other canid types appearing from the fog. I conjectured earlier that these beings might be using the fog or mist to obscure themselves from sight so that they could hunt in the ambush style. The fact that these beings keep appearing to humans should give one pause.

We may also want to consider the idea that these canids are materializing from the fog or mist as per legends unearthed by Linda Godfrey, in *The Beast of Bray Road.*

The author notes that there is significant folklore around werewolves in Dane County, Wisconsin. In these legends, settlers would see wolves appear suddenly and run alongside sleighs in the winter. These wolves could be distinguished from normal wolves by the fact that they disappeared "in a cloud of dust or mist". These disappearing werewolves were considered a bad omen that evil was about to overtake the witness or his or her family.

One presumes that if these supernatural wolves disappeared in a fog, then they might just have appeared in the same way.

This idea is borne out further by a classical werewolf tale told by Sabine Baring-Gould. In Armenia:

> A man once saw a wolf, which had carried off a child, dash past him. He pursued it hastily, but was unable to overtake it. At last he came upon the hands and feet of a child, and a little further on he found a cave, in which lay a wolf-skin. This he cast into a fire, and immediately a woman appeared, who howled and tried to rescue the skin from the flames. The man, however, resisted, and, as soon as the hide was consumed, the woman had vanished in the smoke.

Again, we see a werewolf disappearing into smoke, so one must wonder if the process couldn't be reversed. We will also, later in the text, see witch-finders using fire to discover witches.

To round out this idea further, we turn to Nick Redfern in his *There's Something in the Woods.* Redfern tells the story of Solomon, who encountered a lycanthrope in the woods near Orange, Texas, in 1933.

The boy was fishing with some friends along a "small stretch of water" when he and his two friends developed a strong feeling of being watched. They looked up to find a "large wolf-like head peering through the foliage ..." at them, and their inquisitiveness turned to terror.

According to Solomon, after a few minutes spent glaring at them and pacing along the water's edge, the animal sat down on the ground and began to shake in a rapid, "vibrating" fashion. As it did so, a curious green fog enveloped the wolf, after which it bizarrely, and incredibly, rose up on its hind-legs and backed away into the dense trees. That prompted the young friends to run for their respective homes as quickly as they could. Almost two years passed before Solomon dared venture into the mysterious woods of Orange, Texas again.

This incredible story gives us another piece of the puzzle if we care to believe it. The "curious green fog" seems to have been related to the odd vibration that overtook this creature and seemed to prompt its movement onto its hind legs and away into the dense woods. We will see plenty more examples of strange smells, odd vibrations and other phenomena associated with fog and mist as we proceed.

Interestingly, Orange, Texas, is located in or near (depending on who is drawing the map) the Big Thicket region of Texas, a heavily forested area that is known for Sasquatch sightings as well as ghost lights and other high strangeness phenomena.

Cryptid canines are not the only creatures associated with fog, however. Sasquatch, too, have a strong association with mist and fog, and we will begin our perusal of these accounts in an unlikely spot – the United Kingdom.

SASQUATCH

Linda Godfrey, in her book *Monsters Among Us*, gives us an interesting glimpse into the thinking of the Ho-Chunk First Nations people about everyone's favourite cryptid, Sasquatch. I will save those thoughts for the conclusion of the book, but as someone with a more animistic way of looking at the world, I can accept the Ho-Chunk's thoughts on this matter more easily than some in the field. Part of my reason for such acceptance is that when we begin to look at the relationship between fog and mist and the Hairy One, we fall, almost immediately, into the realm of high strangeness.

Let's begin our examination in the highlands of Scotland.

Ben MaćDhui is the second tallest mountain in the Highlands at over four thousand feet, and it is allegedly "haunted" by a creature that brings terror into the hearts of mountaineers. Lon Strickler, of *Phantoms and Monsters*, gives us several tales of the Grey Man said to live there. Strickler begins with Professor Norman Collie, a respected climber, who related his experience of *Fear Liath Mor* (Big Grey Man in Scottish Gaelic) to his mountaineering club.

In 1925, the professor had summited the mountain and was

returning in mist when he began to hear what sounded like footsteps following him, one sound for every three or four steps that he took. Though he engaged in some positive self-talk, the seasoned mountaineer continued to hear the following noises and did something that no climber of any experience would do – he completely lost his head.

As he puts it, he was "seized with terror and took to my heels, staggering blindly among boulders for four or five miles nearly down to Rothiemurchus Forest ..." It is amazing that, given the aforementioned mist, the professor did not become the object of search and rescue efforts after the perilous descent that he describes.

Collie maintained to the end of his days that there was "something very queer about Ben MaćDhui", and he refused to ever visit the mountain again. Professor Collie did not see anything, only heard the crunching footfalls, but I would note that modern-day Sasquatch researchers assume the presence of the Hairy One based on sounds and stone throws, so who are we to gainsay these witnesses.

Later on, during World War II, a mountain rescue worker, who routinely went into the peaks to rescue downed pilots, had an encounter with *Fear Liath Mor* that left him shaking in the mist.

Peter Densham was at the top of Ben MaćDhui when, once more, a heavy mist fell. Experienced in rescue work, the man took a seat and waited for visibility to improve but then suddenly felt a presence close by. Again, he did not see anything in the thick mist, but he was suddenly seized with panic. Despite his experience in rescue work, the witness took off like a rabbit, coming dangerously close to a cliff and only barely avoiding it. Oddly, he reports that "I tried to stop myself and found this extremely difficult to do. It was as if someone was pushing me. I managed to deflect my course but with great difficulty".

The witness would later say:

> ... tell me that the whine [a sound that he heard as the encounter occurred] was but the result of relaxed eardrums, and the Presence was only the creation of a mind that was accustomed to take too great an interest in such things. I shall not be convinced. Come, rather, with me at the mysterious dusk time when day and night struggle upon the mountains. Feel the night wind on your faces, and hear it crying amid rocks. See the desert uplands consumed before the racing storms. Though your nerves be of steel, and your mind says it cannot be, you will be acquainted with that fear without name, that intense dread of the unknown that has pursued mankind from the very dawn of time.

It appears that Densham not only heard the crunching sounds of footsteps on the rock of the mountain but also heard a vocalization. Again, modern-day Sasquatch researchers might jump on this as evidence of a Hairy One if this story were being told about a mountain in the Pacific Northwest. The British Isles are generally accepted as being too populous, with not enough forest land left, to support a population of Sasquatch-like creatures.

Personally, I find this feeling of panic that seized both men interesting. Some researchers posit that Sasquatch creatures have infrasound capabilities, similar to those used by tigers to paralyze their prey, that produce this terror reaction, presumably to remove *Homo sapiens* from their territory. That's a nice conjecture but not, I think, the only way of looking at this. Some of the subsequent stories will give us plenty of fodder for speculation.

Our final *Fear Liath Mor* experience also occurred during the war years, in 1943, when mountaineer Alexander Tewnion not only met the Grey Man but actually tried to shoot him. The climber related his story in *The Scots Magazine*, which *Phantoms and Monsters* cites.

Tewnion was on a ten-day leave, climbing solo in the Cairngorms. As it was wartime and rations were short, the man carried a pistol so that he could avail himself of any game he might encounter. He had summited Ben MaćDhui when, as with the other accounts, mist swirled and socked the mountain in. Whether it was the weather or something more, Tewnion does not mention, but he notes that the "atmosphere became dark and oppressive" and that the wind picked up.

Climbers dread storms, and fearing that one was about to strike, Tewnion moved quickly to a path down the mountain. As he fled down the slope, making good time, the mountaineer began to hear the telltale crunch of footsteps placed at long intervals behind him. Of course, Professor Collie's story flashed through his mind, but the professor had not been armed, so Tewnion took some comfort in the revolver in his pocket.

The climber said, "A strange shape loomed up, receded, came charging at me! Without hesitation, I whipped out the revolver and fired three times at the figure. When it still came on, I turned and hared down ..." As with the other men in the stories above, Tewnion proceeded at a breakneck pace down the mountain, and as with the others, one must note that it is a minor miracle that he made it off those slopes in one piece.

Interestingly, the mountaineer notes that he returned to Ben MaćDhui a number of times after this event, even travelling in the mist, and had no other events. Perhaps the Grey Man, having scared him off the mountain once, figured that it would be bad form to do it again?

Scotland is not the only place on the British mainland to

have a large, humanlike figure haunting the mists-covered mountains. In Wales, there is a legendary figure called *Brenin Llwyd*, the Grey King, also known as the Monarch of the Mists. This old one is said to be an ancient spirit of the earth that haunts Snowdon, Cader Idris, Plinlimmon and other Welsh mountain fastnesses. This spirit is said to summon the mountain mists and send them to hinder unwary climbers, causing them to lose their way and, perhaps, plunge over unseen cliffs. As with many of the faery, Brenin Llwyd was reputed to be a child stealer.

Lest we think, however, that this is just another quaint faery story, or perhaps a myth that evolved to explain climbers who came to a bad end, there is at least one person who claims to have taken a picture of the Grey King.

In 2008, Gwyn Weeks of Tredegar, Wales, took his dog for its regular walk in the environs of St. James Park when he heard something moving in the underbrush. According to *Wales Online*, the retired steelworker said, "It sent a shiver up my spine, my dog started barking, you could have knocked me down with a feather."

Though the man noted that his eyesight was not good, he did have the presence of mind to whip out his cell phone and take several seconds of video on the device. He used the phone to zoom in on what he was seeing, thinking that he might be encountering one of the legendary alien big cats of Britain but quickly realized that it was something "more like a bear, it was quite ape-like. It could have been a yeti!"

The website notes that the footage shows what appears to be "an animal resembling a gorilla", which seemed to be foraging before standing on its hind legs and walking off into the trees. Weeks reacted as many would and fled in his car straightaway.

While there is no mist or fog mentioned in this story, it does give one pause. Perhaps the Grey King saw fit to come down out of the mountains for a while? In any event, I found it interesting that the postscript to this article had a Crime and Disorder Reduction Officer stating that he was unsurprised by this report and that police would investigate the incident. The constable is quoted as saying, "We take reports of yetis quite seriously ..." and that, "the neighbourhood policing team will be upping patrols and will do their best to persuade the yeti to go elsewhere".

The town is surrounded by hills and mountains. Perhaps the local constabulary are used to seeing "yetis" and other creatures of the mist in their town?

Before we move back to the United States, Nick Redfern, in the first *Wood Knocks* anthology, gives us another story with echoes of the Grey Man and the Monarch of the Mist.

The witness was a boy, out with his friend, investigating one of the many aircraft wrecks from World War II on the Bleaklow Plateau in the Derbyshire Peak District of England. The incident occurred in the early 1960s and began when the witness' friend cried out suddenly. The witness goes on to recount:

> I looked and saw, all in one instant, grouse exploding out of the heather towards us, sheep and hares stampeding towards us and behind them, rolling at a rapid rate towards us from the direction of Hern Clough, a low bank of cloud or fog but what was truly terrifying was that in the leading edge of the cloud bank – in it and striding purposefully towards us – was a huge shadow-figure, a man-like silhouette, but far bigger than a man, as high as the cloud bank, as high as a house. And the terror that hit me and was driving the birds and the animals and my friend was utterly overwhelming – like a physical blow – and I have never felt the like since!

As with our hapless witnesses at Ben MaćDhui, the two boys fled in “mindless terror”, accompanied by all the wildlife of the area. This percipient states clearly that, looking back on the terrain, he wonders how he and his friend did not “break our necks”. Oddly, when the two boys had careered halfway down the mountainside, they “seemed to run out into sunlight”, and the panic disappeared completely. Additionally, sheep, which had been following them in their headlong flight down the mountain, stopped, put their heads down and began to graze as “everything returned at once to normal”.

Ominously, however, when the boys looked back up the mountain, they noted that the “mists were still coiling around” the top of the peak.

As I noted, some Sasquatch researchers believe that the creatures have an infrasound capability that induces this state of terror in witnesses. I find it odd, however, that these phenomena in Scotland, Wales and England all seem to be wound up with fog and mist and equally mysterious that all these witnesses made it off mountainsides in one piece despite flying in obvious horror from their encounter. Only Peter Densham seems to have come close to going over a cliff, and even he managed to avoid the fall.

Let’s move now to the US and more tales of the weird.

When we come to examine the juncture between what John Keel liked to call Big Hairy Monsters and mists or fog, we jump, once more, right into the world of high strangeness. I found it interesting that, though I looked through a large number of references that supported the flesh-and-blood hypothesis of Sasquatch – the Big Man is a relict hominid or unknown species of ape – I seldom found records of mist or fog mentioned in sightings. If these phenomena were mentioned, they were only mentioned peripherally. As soon as I moved to look at sources on the other side of the Sasquatch question, weird mists abounded.

As I've noted elsewhere, I believe in both/and thinking. I see no reason to doubt that the cousins of *Gigantopithecus* or some other physical creature haunt the forests of the world. That thought, however, does not exclude the idea that there may be something a whole lot stranger going on in some of the sightings on record. I feel that a good researcher needs to keep both these possibilities and more in mind.

Having said that, let's look at some of the foggy weirdness associated with the Hairy One.

Joshua Cutchin, in his *Thieves in the Night,* gives us an early story. In July 1888, two-year-old Florence Hughes vanished from her home in Bradford, Pennsylvania. The child had been playing outdoors, and the abduction was blamed on a "wild man" (the terminology for Sasquatch before that term or Bigfoot became commonplace) seen in the area shortly beforehand. When searchers went to look for Florence, a phenomenon familiar to readers of the Missing 411 series popped up – a pervasive fog. Apparently, the fog was so dense that it hampered search efforts. Unfortunately, the Hughes child was never seen again.

Reader, please note that the faery are well known for causing mist and fog to obscure their presence from those seeking them. I am not saying that the "wild man" was a faery being, but in a natural setting, that is certainly an idea I would entertain.

Cutchin and his co-author, Timothy Renner, in their *Where the Footprints End, Volume 1,* tell the story of Larry Abbott. He and two others were checking out noises outside their Point Isabel, Ohio, farmhouse in 1968. The group spotted a "ten-foot tall, four-foot-wide beige hairy creature with glowing eyes ..."

Abbott claimed that the being altered the group's mental

state for a moment, inducing a trance, before someone went to get a rifle. The witnesses claim to have fired on the creature three times. It's not known whether they actually hit the thing since the Hairy One was surrounded in mist and disappeared.

This account is interesting not just for the mist that springs up and into which the being disappears but also for the glowing eyes. In a discussion with Tim Renner on his podcast *Strange Familiars*, we talked about his checklist for high strangeness events, and glowing eyes appear prominently on his list. By the time this volume is at an end, I believe Mr. Renner may have to add mysterious mists to his list of signs that an entity encountered is something more than a physical being.

In another Ohio encounter from the same source, Cutchin and Renner cite the now out-of-print book *Night Siege*. In 1981, at a farm in Rome, Ohio, researcher Dennis Pilichis witnessed a "dramatic series of UFO-Bigfoot sightings".

In one of these incidents that did not appear to involve a UFO, on 3 July, "a strange fog" descended on the farm and its accompanying farmhouse. Two "dark figures" emerged onto a farm field. As with the Abbott story, one of the creatures came under fire and appears to have been hit, shrieking, falling down and then rising to flee. The other being escaped into the tree line, leaving behind a track line of three-toed footprints.

The authors do not give us the context for believing these creatures were Sasquatch, but we can extrapolate. We know that three-toed tracks have been found in other Hairy One sightings and that, supposedly, such tracks are in themselves anomalous. What we don't know is why Sasquatch or Sasquatch-like creatures would seem to be materializing out of a "strange fog".

The *Footprints* books also give us the strange story of a Hairy One of a different colour. As hard as it is to believe, the members of the Wairakei International Golf Course in New

Zealand reported seeing creatures "about two meters in height, slim, and coloured bright green, and with a luxuriant growth of hair". If that wasn't astounding enough, these beings apparently materialized from mist and did so on several occasions.

I had honestly never heard of a bright green Hairy One before. I must wonder, like Lyle Blackburn in his book on the Lizard Man of Scape Ore Swamp, if these creatures hadn't taken a dunk in the local swamp and were covered in algae. Or perhaps these are beings from Elsewhere and this is their native colour?

To make the high strangeness even stranger, Cutchin and Renner go on to outline two cases in which Sasquatch were seen to be floating. In 1975, several witnesses testified to seeing a Sasquatch floating in the air before the creature disappeared into a "strange mist". Later, in 2001, a witness in Chile sighted what the authors describe as a Littlefoot (presumably something like the Orang Pendak of Malaysia or perhaps a juvenile Sasquatch). This particular entity was flying at a high rate of speed and left a trail of grey smoke behind it.

Let's move away from the green creatures and aerial displays and set our feet back on terra firma for the last story in this section. I include this story because there is mist relevant to the story but also because it serves as a fine example of an effect that we will see repeatedly throughout the text. Noted UFO researcher Jenny Randles calls it the "Oz Effect", and I think you will see why.

This tale comes to us from the author W. J. Sheehan as he recounted the story to Wes Germer on the podcast *Sasquatch Chronicles.*

14 September 2014 started out as a normal day for the witness, a Tennessee bow hunter. The subject was off to hunt deer in one of his favourite areas, a densely wooded depression where he had a tree stand twenty-five feet in the air. After

ascending the climbing pins and settling himself into the stand, the hunter propped his back against the tree and looked down into the mist-shrouded bowl filled with trees and underbrush.

The witness states that, due to the mist, he could see no more than seventy-five feet in any direction. As he sat, waiting for his prey to pass into visual range, he became aware of owls calling in the brush. The hunter says that he had the distinct impression, given the number of calls and their location, that the sounds were not made by real owls. The witness, who was an inveterate bow hunter, reported that he found himself wishing for a rifle instead of his trusty bow. He describes feeling a chill, a shiver run through his body and felt his emotions slipping out of his control.

The owl sounds continued to escalate – the man described the noise as sounding like a war party in the fog – and the hunter considered abandoning the hunt and returning to his vehicle. He was so frightened that he chose to stay where he was, however, reasoning that he was safer up the tree than on the ground, running for his car.

It might be that the witness' instincts were correct. He reports that something grabbed his left boot heel, and he turned to stare down into the grimacing face of a gigantic Sasquatch. The creature was described as grey and white with dark skin on its face and chest.

As might be expected, the startled man jumped, and the creature released his foot, standing beneath him and swaying in the manner so often described by Sasquatch witnesses.

The witness considered putting an arrow in the giant, fully expecting the huge beast to pull him and his tree stand out of the tree at any moment. He felt that the owl sounds had been a distraction to allow the Sasquatch to sneak up on him and noticed an eerie silence in the forest as he sat, mind racing, trying to think what to do. After some moments, the giant creature turned and walked off, disappearing into the mist.

The hunter was so terrified that he admits he lost bladder control, and he was unable to get himself to come down from the tree stand for two hours. He finally started down the climbing pegs at 0930, and it was then that he noticed another odd effect – time seemed to slow down. He states that it took him twenty minutes to make the descent from the tree and then another two hours to walk the half mile to his vehicle.

Now, there are several interesting aspects of this case. As I noted earlier, ufologist Jenny Randles coined the phrase "Oz Effect" to describe a specific set of effects that she saw repeatedly in UFO witnesses. Those interested in the paranormal will recognize these effects as well. Randles, in an article in the MUFON UFO journal, gives the following as details of the Oz Effect:

1. Witnesses experience a strange sensation prior to the incident, what could be described as mental tingling and the awareness that something is about to happen.
2. All ambient noise fades away or, at least, fades into the background.
3. The experiencer would have a feeling that time has been affected. Either time seems to slow down or lose its meaning or simply seems not to exist.

We see all of these effects in this Tennessee bow hunter case, and I shall return to Randles and her theories later in the book. For now, be aware that we will see these effects again.

We have to note, too, the size of this Sasquatch. The creature that the hunter describes would have had to be fourteen or fifteen feet tall with seven- or eight-foot arms to reach him in his seat. Many researchers in the field place this size well out of the realm of possibility even for what they consider an adult male Sasquatch.

In the conclusion to this volume, I will discuss why I think that these size limitations are simply theory and may not, in fact, hold for the Hairy One.

In the meantime, let's move on to even more cryptids in the mist.

FLYING THINGS

Most of the beings that we have talked about so far, despite their habit of using mists and fogs for cover, or perhaps even materializing from those mists, are ground dwellers. While tales of beings that fly forth from the fog are not as common, they do exist.

In a legendary account, Linda Godfrey tells us that, according to folklorist William Elsey Connelly, giants used to harass and threaten to exterminate the First Nations Wyandot people in the eastern portion of the US. The Wyandot, of course, fought back and were able to decapitate some of the giants, but this action did not end the threat.

The heads reanimated, bloody hair streaming around their faces, and those heads were known to hide in mist and fog, waiting to "steal children (perhaps with their teeth?) and eat livestock, ruin crops, and cause sickness. Only fire and lightning could kill them.

While some researchers theorize that the giant heads were misperceptions of large owls, I have to call a polite BS on that idea. First Nations people of that time lived on their land and knew the wildlife of the area intimately.

Not only is misidentification unlikely, I know of no owl in the US large enough to carry off a child. I suspect that this is another example of the white, European academics telling us that the people indigenous to an area were superstitious savages and we needn't listen to them. Academia seems to only now be getting over that misapprehension.

Ken Gerhard, in his book on flying humanoids, relates the story of Vladimir Klavdiyevich Arsenyev, the leader of a scientific expedition in the Sikhote-Alin mountains of Russia. The scientist was mapping and documenting the unexplored and temperate wilderness for the Russian Geographical Society and ended up writing a trilogy of popular books detailing his adventures. The incident below was published in the 1937 volume, but we have no exact date for the sighting.

Arsenyev was walking a trail with his dog when he encountered what he took to be human sign. The dog, as is often the case in high strangeness encounters, began to growl and act as though something were wrong. It seemed that there was a large animal moving and stopping in the brush, but because of the humidity and dense fog, the explorer could not make out what was making the noise.

To this point, one might think that Arsenyev had encountered the Almas, the Russian version of a Sasquatch, but the incident took an even harder turn to the strange when the explorer picked up a rock and threw it into the brush, trying to flush whatever was moving there. He succeeded, much to his dismay.

Then something happened that was quite unexpected. I heard the beating of wings. Something large and dark emerged from the fog and flew over the river. A moment later it disappeared into the dense mist. My dog, badly frightened, pressed itself to my feet.

Arsenyev stated that the creature emitted a shriek or howl as it departed.

As you might expect, the geographer was puzzled and spoke about his encounter at dinner that evening. A local tribesman told the story of a "man who could fly in the air. Hunters often saw tracks, tracks appeared suddenly and vanished suddenly, in such a way that they could only be possible if the man alighted on the ground, then took off again into the air".

Note, please, that here is another trained observer who saw something bursting from the mist and flying overhead that he could not explain.

Trevor Constable, in his classic *Sky Creatures*, takes us to the roof of the world, Mount Everest and a peculiar phenomenon sighted by climbers there. Climber Frank Smythe wrote that he was convinced that his sighting was not an optical illusion. He was climbing approximately two hundred feet above Camp 6 (roughly 27,600 feet by the climber's reckoning) and glanced at the North Ridge. He saw:

> ... two curious-looking objects floating in the sky. They strongly resembled kite balloons in shape, but one possessed what appeared to be squat, underdeveloped wings, and the other a protuberance suggestive of a beak. They hovered motionless, but seemed slowly to pulsate, a pulsation incidentally much slower than my heartbeats, which is of interest supposing that it was an optical illusion ... The two objects were very dark in color, and were silhouetted sharply against the sky or possibly a background of cloud ...

The experienced climber was all too aware of the effect that high altitude can have on the senses and put himself through a series of mental tests to be certain that he was seeing what he thought he was seeing. Unable to debunk his own sighting, Smythe started to return to his ascent when "a mist suddenly drifted across. Gradually they [the objects of the sighting] disappeared behind it, and when a minute or two later it had drifted clear, exposing the whole northridge once more, they had vanished as mysteriously as they had come".

It's not at all clear what both Arsenyev and Smythe saw. We do not have enough detail of the sightings to even conjecture, but both men, despite professional reputations to maintain, reported their encounters. Something about whatever they saw was impactful enough for them to be unable to shrug the incident off and go on with their lives.

The same can be said of four Philadelphia, PA, police officers who had a bizarre encounter in South Philadelphia. This incident, too, comes from the files of Trevor Constable. I might have placed the incident in my UFO notes except for the aftermath of the encounter.

Patrolmen John Collins and Joseph Keenan spotted what they thought was a parachute settling slowly down ahead of their patrol car. They reported that it was at the level of the treetops and seemed to be about six feet in diameter and then settled in a field nearby. The officers called for a supervisor, and Sergeant Joseph Cook and Patrolman James Casper responded.

All four officers cautiously approached the object and stood a few feet from it, turning their flashlights on it. The mass gave off a purple glow, "almost a mist, that looked as though if [*sic*] contained crystals".

One of the officers attempted to pick the thing up, but when he placed a hand on it, that part of the mass dissolved. Within twenty-five minutes, the entire substance had dissipated, leaving a "slight, odourless sticky residue". The sergeant was puzzled enough to notify local federal law enforcement, but there was really nothing left for anyone to take samples of or analyze in any way. The officers noted that the thing was so light it did not even bend the weeds on which it landed.

As I noted, I don't even know what to make of this account. The story is one of those delightful Fortean tales that leaves one scratching one's head and wondering what more could come out of the mist or produce a mist as this object did.

In her book *American Monsters*, Linda Godfrey gives us the answer: pterosaurs!

Some people are very dedicated to their sports. I have known runners who would go out even in a Georgia thunderstorm or ride bicycles long distances in the Arizona heat. The witness in this account, surfing off the coast of Oregon, is no exception. It had been so cold that the young man had broken ice off his drying wet suit that October morning in 1986. Nevertheless, he and his buddy hit the waves at dawn and began to surf.

First, "thick fog", with a visibility of thirty feet or so, socked the surfers in. Despite the low visibility, the witness was about ten yards offshore in seven feet of water, waiting for a wave to ride in. The young man noted that, at the time, he was six feet tall and solidly built from working in an auto body shop. Nevertheless, something "buffed" him right off of his board.

The surfer stated that there were three creatures and that they did not flap at all but seemed "intelligent and aware". The animals were about six feet over the water, so the witness saw them clearly and described them as about six feet tall, if they had been standing, with an enormous wingspan of sixteen to eighteen feet. The creatures were light grey with orange "fins" on the back of their heads.

The surfer could not ascertain whether these beings had feathers, scales, or skin as they glided off into the fog, headed north.

Interestingly, the witness told Godfrey, "I had strange feelings ... and if I had been in one of these portals I have heard about in these days over the radio, I wouldn't doubt it." Given what we will see later about fog and the so-called Oz Effect, the witness might not have been far off the mark. Either that, or there is an extant nest of pterosaurs on the coast of Oregon.

It's also interesting to note that it seemed as though no one else on the beach, including this young man's surfing partner, appeared to see this incredible sight. The witness puts it down to the dense fog, but one must wonder. Could this have been a spontaneous psychic event that took this young man, momentarily, into the Earth's past?

Now that we have had a chance to look at the interface between cryptids and fog or mist, let's shift into a discussion of beings that seem to take a less solid form and that might be classified as spirits.

SECTION TWO

PHANTOMS IN THE MIST

VAMPIRES

As we make our transition from cryptid creatures to other areas of high strangeness, let's make a pit stop in the lore of one of the legendary monsters that has a strong association with fog and mist: the vampire.

In his book about shapeshifters, Nick Redfern makes the assertion that the vampire has the strange ability to "shift into a form of fog – a usually localized, but always dense and thick, fog".

As we examine this idea, we run into a definite barrier. Very few people in the modern world believe that there is such a thing as a vampire. To the majority of people in the so-called first world, the vampire is a figure of superstition and a being that one only sees on a movie or television screen.

As someone who has been steeped in esoteric lore for literal decades, I have never believed in the sort of undead vampire portrayed in the movies. However, this doesn't mean that the vampire doesn't have its origins in occult fact. In his terrific work *Monsters: An Investigator's Guide to Magical Beings*, John Michael Greer outlines the occult origins of the vampire mythos.

Greer, a noted Golden Dawn Magician and Druid elder, tells us that:

> Some folk traditions hold that vampires physically leave their graves and stalk through the night, in much the same way as their Hollywood equivalents, but this view seems to be a minority one. More common is the idea that what leaves the grave is a good deal less solid: a cloudy, blurred shape, tangible but soft to the touch. One source in this latter tradition describes the vampire as being like a leather sack full of blood, featureless except for red, glowing eyes ...

According to Greer, in order to understand the legend and lore of the vampire, we have to understand the esoteric view of death. To understand the magician's view of death, we must understand that, in the magical world view, you are not simply the collection of water and chemicals that comprise your physical body. You do, of course, have a physical body, but you also have what some traditions call an etheric body, what you might think of as the energetic matrix upon which the physical body is built. There are other energetic bodies, but they are not really germane to this discussion.

In the occult [hidden from view] way of looking at the world, the death of the physical body and shutdown of its functions is the first death. There is also a second death where the etheric body breaks down and the essence of this person is allowed to move on to an afterlife experience.

A vampire, in this context, is one who has eluded the second death, the breakdown of its etheric substance, by using "debased" magical techniques to utilize the etheric energy of the living to maintain its existence. While blood is certainly a carrier of that etheric energy, the vampire does not need a bleeding victim to steal this energy.

When we look at the folklore of the vampire in the Slavic regions where it seems richest, Jan Perkowski tells us in *Vampires of the Slavs* that the gypsies had a strong belief in the vampire. According to them, "this being is horrible, its hair reaches the ground and when it moves it has a filmy appearance: inside the 'picture' is seen 'just as you paint it', but outside it is 'like a mist'".

Agnes Murgoci, another noted vampire scholar, does not give a direct link between vampires and mist in her *Folklore* article but does mention that the vampire cannot be stopped by simply locking a door. Instead, the vampire may then enter via "the chimney or the keyhole". We can infer from the keyhole reference that the vampire is then able to assume a vaporous form to enter a building not guarded by the traditional remedies of the region, such as garlic.

Additionally, the idea that vampires travel as a fog or mist may also derive from Slavic magical ideas about the vampire. In a somewhat confusing quote, Perkowski relays a statement from a villager from Fenes:

> Every person is a strigoi. A person can be rain, hail, wood, a tree, cow, or an ox, a sheep or a pig. When that person dies, the one who was rain brings on torrents when he dies. The one who was hail brings on a hail storm. The [one] who was a cow causes the cows to die, etc.

Now, typically, when we see this word *strigoi*, it is referring to a vampire, but in this instance, *strigoi* seems to refer to a spirit ally or power that travels with a person, somewhat like the fetch of traditional witchcraft. If each person has one of these powers attached to them, then it makes sense that some might die and become fogs. This idea, combined with the above idea that the vampire could access a home through the keyhole, along with encounters with the etheric revenants discussed above, might be the origin of the idea of vampires converting to mist.

While most of the vampire encounters in the Romanian and Slavic lore are, like werewolf stories, legendary, we do know that the belief in these beings was deep seated in Wallachia, the home of Vlad Tepes, the Impaler, upon whom many believe Dracula was based. Bacil Kirtley tells us, in his article "Dracula: The Monastic Chronicles and Slavic Folklore" gives us this hair-raising bit of history:

> In the monastery at Kirill-Belozersk, in northern Russia near the Finnish border, was found a manuscript which dates from the year 1490 and which is a copy of a document originally penned in 1486. The manuscript relates the story of Dracula ... Which is the name bestowed in horror by monkish chroniclers upon Vlad Tsepesh, Governor of Wallachia from the years 1456 to 1462 and again in the year 1476 ...

The story of Tepes/Dracula was so widely circulated that Kirtley says it was included in a sort of encyclopedia called *Cosmographia Universa* in 1541. The belief in vampires was so deep in that area that, in 1756, the empress Maria Theresa was forced to dispatch officials to Wallachia "for the purpose of investigating a vampire panic and reassuring the populace".

Interestingly, Stoker's fictional vampire sometimes "appear[ed] in the form of phosphorescent specks". Kirtley notes that Romanian vampires often "[came] as points of light shimmering in the air". We will encounter illuminated mists more than once in this text.

Now, dear reader, let me put your mind at ease. While it is possible for someone with that "debased" magical knowledge to create the etheric revenant that we know as a vampire, encountering such a creature in the developed regions of the world is highly unlikely. One of the essentials, as recognized by the ancient Egyptians, for the survival of the etheric body past the first death is an intact physical body.

The Egyptians, of course, took great pains to preserve the corpses of those who could afford the mummification process, but such care of a body is unheard of in the industrial West. Here, human bodies have the blood drained from them and replaced with toxic chemicals as soon as is practicable, and they are placed in the ground in sealed coffins lined with metal. All of these processes would serve, according to Greer, to disrupt the etheric pattern of a body.

Cremation, too, has become a popular way of disposing of the dead, and again, if there is no physical body, there can be no revenant.

Vampire witness accounts that are not legendary may be hard to come by, but while we are in the twilit half-world of negative spirits, let's look at another being said to manifest in smoke: the djinn.

DJINN AND NEGS

First of all, let me be clear that I do not subscribe to the theory that djinn are the producers of all paranormal phenomena any more than I think this is true of demons. What people who propose these theories fail to realize is that the spiritual ecosphere is as dense and varied as the biological ecosphere in our consensual reality. In my animist worldview, every natural feature has a spirit attached, and there are a vast panoply of spirits existing in what we might call the Otherworld.

The djinn are a "species" of spirit that seem to be particularly indigenous to the area of the Middle East, North Africa and other areas of that region, but with the diaspora of humans from those regions, they seem to have travelled elsewhere. One of the things that I find interesting about the djinn is that their existence is taken as a matter of faith by the world's Muslims, and they have their own Sūrah (section) in the Quran.

I tell the story in my book *Phantom Black Dogs: Walkers of the Liminal Way* of an Islamic neighbour of mine who was deathly afraid of my black border collie mix. It took me a while to understand that this person associated black dogs, of any sort, with the djinn since a black dog is one of their favourite forms. I ended up negotiating with the neighbour so that, if she was in the hall, I would wait until she cleared the area before I brought my dog out.

The djinn are supposed to be beings of "smokeless fire" created before humankind, but we see smoke associated with them in some of the legends and witness accounts about them. Robert Lebling, whose *Legends of the Fire Spirits* is essential reading for anyone interested in these spirits, gives us this legend of the classic djinn in a bottle. I will remind readers that these tales are often couched in the context of Islam:

> Abdul Malik, Umayyad caliph in Damascus, was amazed to receive a reliable report that a fisherman on the African coast had recovered in his nets a bottle of brass, stopped with lead and sealed with the signet ring of Sulaiman ibn Da'ud (King Solomon son of David). When the fisherman broke open the bottle, witnesses said blue smoke poured forth and rose into the sky. A horrible voice cried out, "Repentance! Repentance! O Prophet of God!" Suddenly the smoke coalesced into a huge and frightening person, high as a mountain, who just as quickly vanished into thin air.

One of the local rulers further explained the incident by noting that King Solomon, who in legend is a noted magician in addition to being the wise man of the Judeo-Christian scriptures, was incensed against the djinn, presumably because of their refusal to work on the building of the Temple in Jerusalem. Solomon is said to have locked the djinn in bottles and sealed the containers with lead as a punishment, so when the djinn were found and accidentally released, their first action was to repent their sin to avoid being bound again.

In more modern times, Lebling tells us of the Czech explorer

Alois Musil who discovered a djinn haunted ruin during his exploration of the Jordanian desert in 1908–1909. Musil was about fifty miles east of Amman when he came across the ruin and reported:

> ... the sun, just rising, flooded [nearby mountains'] yellow slopes with its rays and made them appear as if they were sprinkled with gold. Before them to the northwest showed the ruin of al-Khawrana (or al-Kharani, as it is called by the Beni Sakhr), resembling a fabulous castle. From all its sides and corners sparks seemed to blaze forth, surrounding the entire structure with rosy light, which caused it to contrast sharply with the blue of the sky. Suddenly the apparition faded away and a cloud enveloped the castle, for the spirit [jinn] who inhabited it would not brook the gaze of the sons of Adam.

The late Rosemary Ellen Guiley had a djinn encounter of her own, which she wrote about in her book *The Vengeful Djinn*. She begins her story by noting that some Muslims believe that certain areas of the world harbour either single djinni or entire djinn families. One of those places was alleged to be in Oman on the Selma Plateau in "a very remote region known as Majlis al Djinn – the meeting place of the djinn".

Guiley determined to visit this place, and like a scene from an adventure movie, her guides refused to travel without being armed, claiming that there were bandits in the desolate area. Majlis al Djinn was a cave, and the group came upon one of its three entrances. When Guiley shined a light into the cave, it did not illuminate the floor of the vast cavern.

On that first viewing, Guiley spotted a green mist but assumed that it came from a water source in the cave. Cold air was erupting from the entrance, telling the investigator that the cavern was a deep one. As Guiley stood contemplating entering the cave, her guide informed her that she would have to go alone – neither he nor the other member of their party would risk going into the cave.

Gamely, the writer got into a rappelling harness and started a descent into the cave. At about the midway point, "a mist began to rise up", and Guiley thought she could hear human voices coming from the darkness beneath her. Wisely, she halted her descent as the mist took on form below her feet.

The part of the mist she was looking at was not in line with the sun pouring in from the hole above; nevertheless, the mist glowed with a "greenish hue". The writer thought she heard a voice telling her in simple English, "Leave. My place."

Guiley's guide and his companion must have seen what happened because they began talking animatedly above her and then disappeared from the cave opening. Afraid that they might leave her stranded, Guiley climbed out of the cave, where she had been left, suspended, seventy-five feet in the air. When she got out of the cavern, her companions were headed for the car, and she had to yell for them not to leave her.

While Guiley had seen only a vaguely cylindrical mist and thought she heard a voice, the two men insisted that they had seen a djinni form and speak to her. There was no persuasion that Guiley could use to get them to go back to the cave. The two men refused to say another word to her on the way back to town, opting instead to spend the time praying.

Now, this is a remarkable account from a seasoned paranormal investigator. I will note a couple of aspects of this case that grab my attention.

First, the green mist is something that we will encounter in the next section of the book, which deals extensively with the faery. Given that faery beings, in all their vast numbers and types, seem to like to live in certain regions of the world, I often surmise that the djinn are simply the faery beings of their region of the world.

Second, a hint to all you legend trippers, paranormal investigators, and other snoopers after high strangeness. If you are going to a place that has a legendary and folkloric association with a powerful type of spirit and something takes form, telling you to get out, then it might be wise to vacate the premises.

It's one thing to take your chances with whatever is hanging out in the local haunted house, but, in this case, Majlis al Djinn was known to the local people as a place where the djinn gathered. Five minutes' study of the djinn will tell you that, if you anger one, at best, your luck is going to take a turn for the worse. At worst, you might just disappear in the desert and not be seen again.

The Vengeful Djinn also gives us the story of Ben, a man who encountered something Other when he was six and then had contact again later in life. Guiley relates this to the djinn, but I will note that, in this book and her other on the djinn, she treats these spirits as the possible source of a variety of paranormal phenomena ranging from poltergeists to alien abductions.

This encounter could have been with a djinn, but it also has a strong "alien" contact flavour to it. While I am not a proponent of the extraterrestrial hypothesis, I acknowledge that there is a specific form of incursion that has certain earmarks to the abduction experiencer. In Ben's case, it seems to me that some of these earmarks are present, but there are also some strong djinn or demonic elements:

> At the age of six, he once woke up in the middle of the night to see a creature standing at the foot of his bed. He described the entity as tall, with scaly skin that looked like an "alligator" with a green glow around it. He

watched in total terror, too afraid to scream for his parents. The entity then looked at him and said, "In the future, I will come for you again and then we shall talk about how you may serve me." The creature's eyes flashed red. It turned into a cloud of black smoke and went right through the bedroom's closed window without breaking it. As soon as the "smoke" left the room Ben was able to move again. Crying in terror, he screamed for his parents. His parents told him what he had seen was nothing more than a nightmare and that it was not real. He wanted to believe them, but deep down, he knew the visitation really had happened. For the next five years, Ben had to sleep with several night-lights on, as he was dreadfully afraid the "monster" was going to come back for him.

The creature did return, when Ben was in his twenties, and its communication with him follows the contactee pattern. The first communications were very accurate, but then the claims became wilder and wilder with more demands for action from Ben. Eventually, Ben was forced to get psychiatric help, and the drugs he was given stopped the communication.

Again, I am not completely certain that Ben encountered a djinni. While a favourite form of the djinn in lore is that of a snake, I did not come across anything, other than Guiley's work, to tie them to so-called reptilians. The being does disappear in a cloud of black smoke, so a djinni is possible, but we will see smoke and mists tied to UFO occupants in a later section of the book. This is an interesting account, and it is even more interesting to note that the medications Ben was given stopped the communication.

I've long been in favour of the idea that the brain is a

receiver for consciousness and not the source of consciousness itself. While one who believes that consciousness comes from the chemical soup of the brain will argue that the whole experience was simply a brain-based delusion and that the medication altered the chemistry to remove the delusion, there is another possibility. If the brain is a receiver for consciousness, then the addition of medications/chemicals would alter the tuning of that brain, much like turning the dial on a radio. The drugs helped this poor man tune to a different frequency so that he could escape these communications.

Robert Bruce, in his book *The Practical Psychic Self-Defence Handbook,* tells a tale that could well have been a djinn incursion. Bruce writes extensively about astral projection, and rather than assigning names to beings that he encounters in the astral space and perceives as negative, he simply refers to them all as "negs". In this experience, however, Bruce is not simply relating an astral voyage but an encounter that left him with physical injuries.

In this account, Bruce states that he had a friend who seemed to be having trouble with negative presences (see below for my comments on this aspect of the story), and the man was staying with Bruce at the time. The two retired for the evening, but Bruce began to have cramps almost immediately and then slipped into what he calls "real-time astral sight". In his way of working, this simply means that you are seeing with your "astral" eyes and don't need to have your physical eyes open.

In this altered state of consciousness, Bruce noted that "a column of dense, black smoke as thick as a man's leg" was forming over his friend. Bruce reported:

> The column swayed back and forth several times and then struck at me like a snake. It bit my leg and searing

> pain coursed through my left calf muscle. I was temporarily paralyzed and felt a strong sucking sensation on my left leg. A few seconds later I managed to break the paralysis and rolled out of bed.

Bruce applied a number of traditional cures that he says work on "negs" of all types, but when he woke in the morning, he found a "large, puffy swelling at the bite area on [his] left leg". The swelling stayed with him for some time after this incident.

Skipping over the scientific materialists having a cow over this account of an event that happened, at least partially, in an altered state, I think we can say that while this incident might not have had objective reality (I am not certain what I would have seen if I had been standing there), it certainly had subjective reality and that reality had some effect on the man's physical body.

Was this a djinni? We have seen the black smoke in reference to the djinn in stories above, and it is well known that the snake is a favourite form of these spirits, so it is entirely possible. I would be interested to know if the man having issues with negs came from a part of the world where these spirits are extant and, if so, what he might have done to garner their attention.

While we are on the subject of so-called negative spirits, let's take a moment to dissect that. I am not one of those sweetness and light people who believe that all beings of the Otherworld are going to shower us with rainbow sprinkles and gumdrops if we ask them to. There are certainly some beings that actively detest humankind (sometimes with good reason) and will go out of their way to try to harm us.

In my experience though, the vast majority of dwellers on the Otherside don't even pay attention to our antics. They live their lives and are quite willing to let us lead ours unless we do something that disturbs them. In that case, they may make trouble until a human is sensitive enough to put things right or involves a professional to assist.

Some spirits, like the power animals that work with shamans, the spirit guides of spiritualism and angels, have no issue working with human beings and, indeed, seem to have an interest in our spiritual development. Do not make the mistake of thinking that these beings are harmless, however. Remember that, according to the scriptures followed by almost a billion people, angels, for example, are quite capable of taking out an entire army if there is reason to do so.

Remember, too, in any discussion of spirits that their positive or negative qualities are often dependent on our perspective. I mentioned angels as a good example. We might also look at legends of the Wild Hunt as another example.

Universally feared throughout large parts of Europe, the Wild Hunt can be seen, from a magical perspective, as the spirit world's way of cleaning up transient, dross energies in preparation for the winter sleep of the Earth. Whether the Hunt is good or bad has entirely to do with perspective and whether you are one of the unfortunates who didn't listen to the stories and ventured out when you shouldn't have.

With these thoughts of perspective in mind, we move on to another set of beings who are intimately associated with mist and fog – the faery – where we will take a look at both historical and modern accounts of the Little People.

THE FOLK: HISTORICAL PERSPECTIVES

Other than ghosts, which we will discuss in a subsequent section, perhaps no other being is more closely associated with fogs and mists than the faery. After tonnes of research in faery lore over many years, I long ago came to the conclusion that the term faery or the Fair Folk or the Little People or any of the hundreds of names assigned to this category of being is a catch-all. One has only to look at Katharine Briggs' extensive work in categorizing the faery of Europe to understand that the faery are not just one being or type of being. They are a vast panoply of spirits who hold humans in various states of regard, and we are going to look at both the historical and modern-day sightings of these beings.

The Scots, for example, divided the faery into the Seelie and Unseelie Courts. This might be a useful way of beginning to look at faery – there are those beings that are willing to work with and co-exist with humans and those beings who are actively hostile to our interests.

I am not a dualistic thinker, however. I would propose that there are a whole range of faery who are indifferent to humans and who adopt a sort of "I won't bother them if they don't bother me" approach to humans. We might call these the wild fae. In my novel *Hunting the Beast,* I proposed the Sasquatch as a form of wild fae, and given some of the stories in the last section, particularly those of the Grey Man and the Monarch of the Mist, I wonder if I might have had a touch of psychism in the writing for that fictional piece.

Be that as it may, we have only to look at Lewis Spence's classic text *The Fairy Tradition in Britain* to discover a relationship between the faery and mist. Spence tells us that:

> The most characteristic among the arts of fairy magic, perhaps, is that of illusion, enchantment, or, to employ its expressive Scottish synonym, glamourie ... The sudden casting of a mist over the landscape by a fairy when pursued is a notion having the same origin.

Katharine Briggs, in her classic study *The Vanishing People,* tells us that the country folk that she studied took their belief in the faery a step further and actually felt that these beings were responsible for growing things. She speaks of a cottager who felt the work of the "bogles" (faery beings of that region) was waking the earth as spring came on and that this work was signified, to her senses, by a green mist that rose from the fields. The witness stated clearly that, upon seeing this mist, the yard would awake again, and that the trees and plants and the seeds would begin to sprout.

We begin to see the ambivalence that those who lived close to the earth had about faery beings. On the one hand, the Folk were tricksy, confusing the senses and hiding in mist and always willing to take offence and make one's life miserable (thus the enormous number of ways to fend off the Folk seen in the folklore). On the other hand, however, people realized that these beings played a vital role in the fertility upon which their very lives depended in those days.

W. Y. Evans-Wentz, in his monolithic study of the fairy faith, brings the relationship of the faery and mist into sharp focus. As was his wont, Evans-Wentz stopped on the road to speak with a woman named Maggie Timmons in the area of New Grange, Ireland. He asked her, after some introductory speech, if any of the "good people" appeared in the region. She replied that she was sure her neighbours used to see them since the faery had "inherited" the local fort.

When the author asked his subject what the "good people" were, she replied:

> "When they disappear they go like fog; they must be something like spirits, or how could they disappear in that way? I knew of people," she added, "who would milk in the fields about here and spill milk on the ground for the good people; and pots of potatoes would be put out for the good people at night."

We see here two aspects of the "fairy faith" that recur throughout Evan-Wentz's enormous study. One is that the Fair Folk are not entirely of this world and are able to make their escape into a fog or mist, and the other is that the humans who lived side by side with them made offerings to ensure the "good people's" continued goodwill. As we proceed, the reader will begin to get a view of why it is so important to stay in the good graces of "Those Ones".

Evans-Wentz tells the story of three women on the Isle of Barra in Scotland, who went out to look after some sheep. The herd was located on a hillside, and that hillside was quickly overtaken by fog. The women, sensibly, sat down upon a knoll and started to sing a song for working cloth. Their singing attracted the attention of one of the Folk, "a fairy woman in the rocks [who] responded to their song with one of her own".

The Fairy Faith in Celtic Countries also gives us the tale of Bill Clarke of the Isle of Man who was fishing from a ledge of rocks one day when a "dense grey mist began to approach the land". Clarke thought he had best make for home while he could still see the path, but as he was putting his things together, he heard a sound like "a lot of children coming out of school".

When the fisherman looked up, he was astonished to behold an entire fleet of faery boats on both sides of the ledge where he stood. Clarke describes the riding-lights of the boats as being like "little stars", and he heard one of the Little People shouting, "Poor times and dirty weather, and herring enough the people of this world, nothing at us". Apparently, despite their mystical abilities, even the Folk have a bad day fishing sometimes.

A final story from Evans-Wentz gives us a view of a legendary figure from the forest of Brocéliande in France. This faery woman had already made a name for herself by refusing to give up the estate upon whose grounds she lived. It was said that the lady in question actually showed up at the auction for the estate and dissolved it into chaos when she made a bid. Of course, no sane person was going to bid against one of the Folk, so the auction dispersed, and the estate remained unsold.

The author of *The Fairy Faith* encountered a woman gathering bundles of sticks for firewood and, as he had all over the Celtic lands, engaged the woman in conversation. She told an interesting story of this same faery woman saving her husband's life.

It was not uncommon, in those times, for a poor man to go onto the property of another, seeking game to feed his family. The woodcutter, in this case, "had one night gone to watch for a roebuck in the neighbourhood of the Butte-aux-Plaintes and had been caught red-handed by a party of keepers". The would-be poacher, of course, sought to get away, and the gamekeepers fired on him, hitting him in the thigh.

The man was prepared to fight and die in order to avoid the ignominy of capture when suddenly "a kind of very thick mist" sprang up and was so thick that one could not see the ground or the trees, much less a fallen poacher.

The wounded man heard a voice coming from the mist, "gentle like the rustling of leaves, and murmuring in his ear: 'Save thyself, my son: the spirit of Vivian [the faery of that forest] will watch over thee till thou hast crawled out of the forest'". The poacher made his escape, and his wife crossed herself in reverence to the faery each time she spoke the benefactor's name.

Lewis Spence, in his work on the "fairy tradition", gives us a Welsh example of a well-known Irish faery being, the bean sí, anglicized as banshee. In the Welsh tradition, the creature is called a *cyhiraeth* and "comes in a dark mist to the window of a person about to die, flapping her wings against the glass, and repeating his or her name". Like the Irish banshee, who incidentally translates to something like "woman of the faery mound", the *cyhiraeth* "gives forth a wailing noise in the night before a death or burial and, if one proceeds to a person's deathbed after hearing the *cyhiraeth*, then the dying person's moans will mimic the cries of the faerie being – one strong cry, one weaker cry and one faint cry."

The *cyhiraeth* was also known as a predictor of shipwrecks where her cries were associated with floating lights, and she was also seen as a predictor of epidemics. Unlike the Lady Vivian, the black mist of the *cyhiraeth* was not something one wished to encounter unless they were ready to see what lies beyond the gateway of death.

Faery stories from folklore often have a moral to them.

Katharine Briggs tells the tale of the Tacksman of Auchriachan near Glenlivet, Scotland, who used the magic taught to him by his grandmother to keep the local faery folk from taking the essence of his food. This, of course, made him unpopular with the local fae, so when the man lost some goats and went looking for them, thick fog settled over him, so thick that he sat down to let it pass.

But as so often happens in these tales, he saw a light and moved toward it only to come upon a "curious dwelling, almost as if a part of the hill had been raised up on pillars". When he knocked on the door, he was astonished to see a woman whose funeral he had attended some months before. One suspects that, at this point, the man knew he had wandered out of his own realm and into another.

The dead woman was an old friend, and when she discovered that he was in a fix, being unable to find his way home through the mist, she hid him in this cottage of the faeries. The owners of the cottage came in hungry, and the Tacksman had to endure listening to them plot to take his ox, his son having forgotten the spell of protection, as well as bread that his wife failed to place a cross on after baking.

The miser (in the faery's view, at least) did finally make it home but was forced to slaughter the ox and dispose of its remains as well as throw the bread by the wayside, where "neither cat nor dog came near them, or indeed all the good had been taken out of them to the fairy knowe".

Another Briggs story also relates to the issue of being stingy with the faery. "An old curmudgeon" bought a farm and almost immediately ordered the servants to stop putting out clean water and a dish of cream for the local fae, called pixies in this story. Things began to go wrong around the farm immediately and culminated with "four fine young heifers" getting lose and leading the farmer a merry chase when he went out to catch them.

Despite his yells for assistance, which went unheard, and his best efforts to catch the heifers, the farmer was thwarted at every turn. When he was finally about to catch up to the livestock, the mist came down to thwart him. After running over hill and over dale most of the night, the farmer surrendered and returned home, "all a-bruised and a-tore and soaked to the bare skin" only to find the heifers securely stored in his barn. Apparently, the four had been in the barn all night.

It doesn't do to fail to give the faery their due in the legends and tales of the past, but lest the reader think that the Little People are no longer extant in the realms of high strangeness, let us look at some more modern witness accounts.

THE FOLK: MODERN-DAY SIGHTINGS

As we have seen, there is a rich history of faery lore, but it is also the case that modern people see the "People of the Mist". Given that modern people do not generally have the knowledge of their faery neighbours that the folk we discussed previously do, one suspects that faery encounters these days are far more fraught, and the following stories will demonstrate that this might be true.

We open our consideration of more modern faery encounters and their misty accompaniment with an incident reported by Linda Godfrey in her book *Monsters Among Us*. Godfrey cites Western Michigan University professor Michael Swords, who recounts the story of a miner in the region of Yellowknife in the Northwest Territories of Canada. This gentleman was on the Coppermine Mountain and was in the act of exploring a fifty-foot-deep gully full of interesting-looking rocks.

The miner came across a tubular mist that, "was distinct from the rest of the atmosphere" and decided to walk into the mist. One questions his sanity with this action, but when he passed through the mist, he found himself wading through three-foot-high grass. Astonished, he experimented and discovered that he could walk back through the mist to the gully and then back to the grassland.

Emboldened by that knowledge, the miner resolved to move farther into this grassy land. He came to a lake, which sat on a hillside, and spotted "two, robed humanoid figures" watching him as they floated several feet above the grass.

Not surprisingly, the miner decided to return to his own world but only managed it with extreme difficulty.

This encounter is important. In subsequent sections of the book, we will see mists and fogs associated with disappearances. Might it not be the case that, in certain circumstances, these fogs are literally doors to the faery realm or other dimensions?

We know from faery lore that entry into the realm of the Little People is not always temporary. It is said, for example, that the Reverend Robert Kirk, the Scots clergyman who wrote *The Secret Commonwealth,* was imprisoned in the faery realms for revealing the secrets of Those Ones. Given what we shall see later and all the ways that these mysterious mists cause confusion, I feel that such a hypothesis is not out of line.

Christopher Pittman, in his online discussions of the Bridgewater Triangle area of Massachusetts, speaks of an area resident who encountered a being that he described as "a small black thing that looked like a midget" high up on the wall of a barn. Just like the faery of old, when this being noticed his regard, it "seemed to disintegrate", moving toward the witness in a mist-like form. The individual, probably wisely, fled but then returned later. He found nothing on his second trip to the barn but did notice "weird screeching noises like a pig" in the area.

According to Janet Bord's, *Fairies: Real Encounters with Little People*, in the Bedfordshire County of England, seven boys, ages ten and eleven, "were playing on Studham Common early in the afternoon of 28 January, as they made their way back to school". Their sighting was preceded by lightning, which startled the group, and subsequent thunder. One of the boys, Alex Butler, saw "a little blue man with a tall hat and a beard" and, of course, pointed this oddity out to his friends. As young boys will do, the group ran toward the being, who then disappeared "in a puff of smoke".

These lads, not to be deterred, started to look about for the little man and soon spotted him again, but he disappeared once more as they got near. On the third try, the group began to hear "deep voices, strange and babbling", but before they could sneak up on the little fellow, they were called in to school.

The little person was described as "about three feet tall and wearing a tall hat or helmet like a bowler without the brim. Details of the being's appearance were obscured by a greyish-blue glow". The boys also reported that the being had a six-inch-square black box mounted on its belt and seemed to have a divided beard. In addition, the boys noted that the little man's "arms were short and held close to the body", but they could not get a clear view of his lower half.

There is some conflict about whether the being was disappearing in a "puff of smoke" or whether the children were targeted by the black device on the being's belt. The boys seemed to think that the "yellowish-blue mist" came from the box and was aimed at them. Bord points out that the mist, which cleared quickly, may have simply hidden the entity from view long enough for it to disappear into the undergrowth. This use of smoke for obscuration is a behaviour we will also see in UFO cases.

Whether the little person was disappearing in a cloud of smoke and reappearing elsewhere or using mist to obscure itself from sight so that it could hide, this seems to be a rather high-tech faery. I was struck, in this story, by the agreement amongst the boys that the little person's lower half was not visible. It brought to mind all the examples of ghostly apparitions that seem to be missing body parts, including the lower body.

In Newfoundland, Canada, the faery display the same tricksy behavior they are famous for in European stories. Barbara Rieti relates the tale of a St. John's man:

> He and a companion got lost when the fog came in and were lost for approximately fourteen days. When they finally managed to come out of the woods they said that the fairies had saved them. He said that every time they wanted to lie down and go to sleep because they were exhausted, a little man with a green suit and red cap would make them keep walking. Other than that, they would have undoubtedly died of exposure because the weather on the 24 of May here in Newfoundland is never too warm ...

Now, this story only peripherally involves fog, but I couldn't help but wonder what and where the fishermen were that they got so lost in the fog that they were missing for fourteen days. One presumes that someone was looking for them in the area where they disappeared.

And how is it that these fellows were able to stay on their feet for fourteen days? If the faery being kept them moving any time they wanted to settle, there is definitely some distortion of time happening in this event. The record for going without sleep is about eleven days, and the subject had "cognitive and behavioural changes ... [which] included moodiness, problems with concentration and short term memory, paranoia and hallucinations".

After fourteen days of sleeplessness, especially in a survival scenario with suboptimal nutrition, etc., the fisherman should have been in terrible condition. There is no indication that this was the case. Instead, it almost seems as though these men walked into the woods and then walked out shortly thereafter, and the fourteen days were spent "elsewhere".

Remaining in Newfoundland, we encounter less happy stories of the fae. Rieti speaks of a woman and her grandchild, in Northern Bay, who disappeared in a fog while berry-picking and were not found until the following spring ... "behind the fence of a garden right in the community, the child was in her arms, they were sitting under a tree".

This story so closely resembles other mysterious disappearances involving fog and mist that we will review later in this work that I wonder if this had anything to do with the faery at all.

We also have the case of a young Bell Island man who encountered what he called the banshee [the bean sí that we ran into earlier in Scottish folklore]. This fellow saw that banshee as "a sort of cloudy mist [humanlike] which appeared only on the full moon of a Wednesday night, and sort of enveloped anyone who happened to meet it ..." The young man banished the being with the sign of the cross before it could enfold him.

I find this story odd since the banshee, in European lore, is the Washer at the Ford, crying out to portend the death of someone, often in a family to which the faery is attached. The being described above may have been called a banshee because the young man had no idea what else to call it. We will see more examples of enfolding clouds later, and given those examples, I am again hesitant to say that this mist that enwraps people is a faery phenomenon.

All paranormalists love a good witness, so when a police officer sees faeries, my attention is immediately riveted. Janet

Bord, in her book on real faery encounters, relates the testimony of Police Constable David Swift. The constable was on early morning patrol in East Hull in the Humberside area of England. He spotted a "bank of fog" over playing fields near Stonebridge Avenue and went to investigate when he spotted three figures dancing on the field.

Thinking they were intoxicated, the constable started to approach the three figures, and they promptly disappeared "into thin air". Swift's description is worth quoting:

> ... a man dressed in a sleeveless jerkin, with tight-fitting trousers ... [the other two were women] wearing bonnets, shawls and white dresses. All had an arm raised as if dancing round an invisible maypole ...

We're not given any detail about the size of these three, but the dancing behaviour is one certainly associated with the faery.

Janet Bord does not just give us evidence from Europe, however. Moving to South America, she notes that, "black, hairy dwarfs" made an appearance to children in Roque Saenz Pena, Argentina, in May and June of 1985 before describing the experience of three children from Parana City, in the same country, in December 1986.

The children, ranging in age from eight to eleven, were entertaining themselves on the bank of a local stream when "eight to ten gnomes appeared as if by magic. They had claws for hands, not much hair and two small horns! Having no feet, they appeared to levitate above the water ..."

The children demonstrated good sense and ran, but one, an eight-year-old named Claudio, tripped and fell. His friends did not stop for him, and the boy threw a stone at an approaching gnome in desperation. The stone zoomed directly through the being, but Claudio was unharmed as the creatures "shrank and disappeared in a cloud of black, sickening smoke".

Oddly, despite not having feet, strange tracks were found in the area after the incident.

In his brief history of supernatural child abduction, Joshua Cutchin tells the tale of Daniel Klemsrud and his girlfriend. The couple were hiking near Boscobel, Wisconsin, in 1995 when they became lost. A "thick mist" settled over the trail they were on, and the couple heard "the sounds of giggling, like small children laughing at play". Klemsrud looked through the foliage and saw two small figures disappearing into "a warren at the base of a hill".

Mr. Klemsrud must have been a bit fey himself, or he was knowledgeable in faery lore. He had an intuitive feeling that he should toss two coins at the mouth of the tunnel where he had seen the figures disappear. As soon as he did this, the mist disappeared, and the trail leading out of the forest was revealed.

Reading this account, one wonders if the mist that appeared was not the proximate cause of the couple becoming lost. As we've noted and seen in this section, fogs and mists are certainly associated with the fae and could even be liminal areas leading to the Land of the Faery.

Finally, Nick Redfern, in an internet article, talked to witnesses who had an explosive experience in Wales associated with little men. The events in this tale were preceded and then followed by "a weird mist [that] came down out of nowhere. This was nothing like a normal mist ..."

Witness Annie Owen and her family were roughing it on a mountain "above Trefriw and Llanrwst near the River Conwy". The couple had purchased a pair of four-hundred-year-old cottages, which they planned to convert, and were camping in a caravan, what Americans might call a travel trailer. They were accompanied by their two children and even had a horse with them.

On the night of 23 January 2000, the horse became very restless and began to rock the caravan. Owen says the beast was in a "terrible state". Looking out the window, presumably to see what the matter was, Owen and her family saw a "white ball, very slow-moving" at an unknown distance. The witness estimated the size of the ball at two to three feet wide but admits that such estimation was difficult due to the blackness of the night.

Suddenly, there was a "colossal" bang.

Odd, but the story does not end there. There was one person on the mountain who was local to them, and this older woman had been awakened by the loud bang. She looked out her bedroom window and spied "little men" who were "very small and all dressed in black – about three or four feet tall". The older woman had seen military on the mountain before and wondered if this sighting had something to do with the armed forces.

Ordinarily, seeing people creeping around in black garb, very early in the morning, might indicate military or police presence, but the size of these individuals – the woman states there were four or five of them – gives one pause. And why would someone who lived on the mountain and knew its meteorological variations make such a fuss over the mist that descended before and after this event. That mist had to have been uncommon enough to attract their attention.

Moving on from Little People slipping in and out of the mist, in our next chapters, we will delve into a phenomenon very often associated with or even comprised of mists: ghosts.

GHOSTS

There are countless reports from ghost hunters and those living in haunted quarters of sighting mists and smelling, if not seeing, tobacco smoke. One has only to stroll through the ghost sites on the internet to get a view of how common such things are, and when we add in the annals of old and respected psychical researchers, the volume of lore multiplies. I did not want to write a book specifically about ghosts, but I did want to include some of the lore, as it does point to the all-inclusive nature of visual obscurations in the paranormal and beyond.

Christopher Balzano, in his *Picture Yourself Ghost Hunting*, addresses the subject of ghostly mists and includes pictures of mists, both explained and unexplained, in his book. As he notes, the presence of mists within a house is almost sure-fire evidence of a ghostly incursion unless one finds that the house is on fire. Outdoor mists and fogs are more problematic since they are just as likely to be environmental as they are to be paranormal. Balzano recommends that mists be photographed, since they may contain sections that are "unnaturally thicker and movement that might be irregular". These signs, Balzano says, are symptoms of paranormal activity.

This connection between mysterious mists and ghosts is so strong that it often leads people who see one of these visual obscurations to make a connection with someone departed. Stephen Wagner, in a liveaboutdotcom article, gives a perfect short example.

My husband and I witnessed a strange phenomenon. We were sitting in our living room. Just then a puff of smoke or fog rushed between us, stopped in front of our faces, swirled up, and quickly vanished. I asked him, "Did you see that?" He responded, "Yes, but I don't know what that was!" We don't smoke ... no open windows. It came out of nowhere. To me it was definitely a spirit. My husband lost his grandmother at the end of October; he was really close with her. I wonder if it was her telling us she's in the afterlife. I would like to know, but I'm not willing to do something to cause my family harm.

While the presence of a mysterious fog in one's living room is certainly puzzling, it did not follow that the mist was the ghost of the husband's grandmother. It could just as easily have been a passing ghost wandering through to some other appointment, or even the incorporeal essence of a local land spirit. Regardless, the witnesses did have an experience with mist that left them puzzled.

In another such event, the strange fog is related to a ghost dog sighting.

Cannock Chase, in England, is a place noted for its high strangeness. Brad Steiger, in his book on real monsters, gives the account of a couple who wrote into their local newspaper upon seeing an article about a ghost dog sighting in their area. The article reminded the two of an incident that had occurred to them in July of 1980 (approximately).

The pair had attended a celebration at a local restaurant and were driving home about 2330 hours. The writer of the letter states that, "We had driven up Coal Pit Lane and were just at one the bends before the approach to the Holly Bush when, from the high hedge of trees on the right-hand side of the road, the headlights picked out a misty shape which moved across the road and into the trees opposite."

Both of the witnesses saw this phenomenon. They reported that the mist had a definite shape, being eighteen inches to two feet deep and nine or ten feet in length. The letter writer also stated that it was a "clear, warm night with no mist anywhere else". Both witnesses, despite knowing nothing of a history of sightings in the area, felt that they had witnessed something paranormal, and the wife remarked at the time that she thought she was looking at a ghost.

Again, there is no indication that this large and peculiar fog formation was a ghost dog or a ghost dog beginning to form. To their credit, the witnesses do state that they are not sure their event was related to the other sightings in the area. Given Cannock Chase's reputation, one wonders what might have materialized from that mist if the witnesses had followed it into the woods.

When we begin to delve into ghost cases, we have to look at the groundbreaking work of Hans Holzer. In his massive compendium of true ghost encounters, Holzer gives several good examples of hauntings that involve mists.

For example, Diane S. was a young woman whom Holzer indicates had no interest in "psychic matters" until age seventeen when the young man she fancied was killed in a car accident. There was a period of time after the funeral when Diane felt that Kerm, her dead friend, was reaching out to her, but these experiences quieted after a while.

By July of 1965, Diane had recovered sufficiently to attract the attention of another suitor, Jerry. One night, after a party, the two stayed up talking until almost dawn before Jerry headed home. As the young man drove past the spot where

Kerm died, he felt moved to stop and get out of his car, ostensibly to stretch his legs. When he got back to the car, it was "enveloped by a thick fog".

Jerry got into the cold, clammy car and looked to his right. A white, cloud-like object crossed the road and approached the car, to Jerry's considerable consternation. The "cloud" was quite clear to Jerry. It held the "blurred image of a human body" and the face of Kerm. A strange voice, like the sound of an echo, told Jerry to "take care of Di".

Kerm's misty hand reached for Jerry, and the lad fainted. Oddly, and we will see this in later sections of the book, Jerry came to parked outside the local graveyard with no idea how he had gotten there.

The story ends with Jerry shakily driving home, but I wonder if the young man continued to court Diane after this or decided that discretion might be the better part of valour.

Holzer also tells the story of Carol S, a new mother who had a non-threatening ghost experience. In 1963, following the birth of her first son, Carol woke to see a "misty light" hanging near the ceiling of the room between the baby's bassinet and the foot of the bed. That light took the form of Carol's grandfather's face, and Carol had the impression that the man had come to see his first great-grandchild.

The face remained floating at the ceiling for a moment and then disappeared into fog before dispersing altogether.

No look into ghosts, fogs and mists or not, would be complete without at least one ghost-on-a-staircase story. In December of 1969, five shop girls in a boutique on High Street, Kent, spotted a ghost on closed-circuit television. According to Holzer, the apparition of a woman in a long Victorian dress seems to have been solid enough at one point to fool one of these young ladies into approaching it.

The shop girl, alerted to a new customer by a colleague

monitoring the closed-circuit TV system, walked right through the woman she had gone to assist. The figure, which had been at the foot of the stairs initially, ascended the stairs, where it "disappeared in a sort of mist and then reappeared again". The sighting happened at lunchtime, but despite five of the staff seeing this apparition on the CCTV, when they went upstairs to investigate, they found nothing further.

Astonishingly, unlike most ghost appearances, this Victorian lady appeared to enjoy her audience and remained visible at the head of the stairs, "waving her hand and patting her hair", for almost an hour. There is some confusion in the account about whether the shop girls were seeing this apparition with their eyes, the closed-circuit TV or both, but it is a fascinating story nonetheless.

The Whaley House is a well-known haunt in San Diego, and Holzer investigated there as well. During a time period when the house was host to a historical re-enactment, there was paranormal activity in play. William Richardson, a member of the cast, recalled that:

> Later in the run of the show, the apparitions began to appear. The cast had purchased a chair which had belonged to Thomas Whaley and placed it in the front parlor. Soon after, a mist was occasionally seen in the chair or near it. In other parts of the house, especially upstairs, inexplicable shadows and mists began to appear. George Carroll swears that he saw a man standing at the top of the stairs. He walked up the stairs and through the man. The man was still there when George turned around but faded and disappeared almost immediately.

William Stead, in *Real Ghost Stories*, gives us a terrific

example of what psychical researchers call a crisis apparition. The witness, Captain G. F. Russell Colt, had a brother, Oliver, serving in the 7th Royal Fusiliers at Sebastopol during the Crimean War. Colt corresponded frequently with his brother, and during a time when the brother had been ill and was feeling down, Colt had written him to raise his spirits but make certain that he appeared to him if something did happen. This seemingly morbid request was not at all uncommon during this time period of growing interest in spiritualism and psychical research.

Unfortunately, the young lieutenant was killed in heavy action on 8 September 1855. The captain reports, "That night I awoke suddenly and saw facing the window of my room by my bedside, surrounded by a light sort of phosphorescent mist, as it were, my brother kneeling." The unexpected apparition, for the captain professed not to really believe in such things, left the man tongue-tied.

Neither was this a dream. The captain rose from his bed, looked out the window and noted the atmospheric conditions before turning to see that Oliver was still there. Being of a sturdy constitution (apparently), the captain tried shutting and opening his eyes and even walking through the apparition to dispel it. Nothing worked, but as the captain went to leave the room, his brother's apparition turned its head, and he saw a wound in the ghost's right temple.

The captain spent the rest of the night in a friend's room in the house, and when he reported his sighting to his father in the morning, he was told to keep quiet for fear of upsetting their mother. It was only upon learning of the particulars of his brother's death that Colt found out that the young soldier had been killed by a gunshot to the right temple.

According to Mason Winfield and his co-authors in *Haunted Rochester*, the spirit of Mary Jemison still haunts Letchworth

State Park in New York, appearing as "a short, columnar mist" (something we have seen on a couple of previous occasions), which moves about the "Gardeau Flats at the rivers' [*sic*] edge as deliberately as if it lived. It disappears as it nears the tree line".

Jemison, known by settlers as the White Woman of the Genesee, led a life of hardship and love. Her childhood family was murdered by a mixed party of French and Shawnee, and Mary was taken captive before being sold to "some Senecas who took her to their village. The child was adopted and named Dehgewanus (roughly: a pretty girl) and eventually married into the tribe as well.

After the French and Indian War, Jemison chose to stay with the Seneca, and to make certain her wishes were kept, she and her Seneca husband fled to a more remote location. Unfortunately, her first husband died of illness, but Mary went on to wed the war chief Hiakatoo, a man said to be "kind and moderate" with his family despite his massive appearance.

Jemison stayed with the Seneca despite years of hardship and the loss of three sons to the white man's fire water. She died in 1833 and was buried amongst the Seneca with her body eventually being moved to a site near her home in the Genesee River Valley.

We've actually trended backward in time for this chapter, so I wanted to close with this interesting note from Karl Shuker in *The Unexplained.*

> Perhaps the most astonishing, and distant, member of Britain's royalty to linger in a contemporary limbo of the lost, however, is none other that [*sic*] Boadicea (Boudicca), Queen of the Iceni, who committed suicide during the first century AD rather than be captured by the Romans. The many centuries that have passed since

> then have created a Britain immeasurably different from the one she knew, but she still has not abandoned it, for a spectacular apparition of this valiant warrior has occasionally been sighted in modern times, emerging from the mist near Ermine Street, a Roman road in Lincolnshire.

I can well imagine this warrior queen assuming the role of a guardian of Britain in her afterlife.

Now that we have talked a little about ghosts and the mysterious mists that are associated with them, let's look at a related topic.

PHANTOM EVENTS

It is one thing for people to have sightings of ghosts that are at least vaguely reminiscent of human beings, but it is quite another thing for our mists and fogs to be associated with other strange, let's call them phantom, events.

Karl Shuker, in *The Unexplained,* gives an assuredly creepy account of a phantom road accident:

> Most eerie of all, however, must surely be phantom road accidents, in which the transport is real, but the victim is a ghost. Driving along the A12 towards Great Yarmouth on the rainy evening of 2 November 1981, Andrew Cutajar was near to Hopton when he saw a grey mist in the middle of the road. As he drew nearer, it resolved itself into the form of a tall long-haired man dressed in a long coat or cloak and wearing old-fashioned lace-up boot[s]. The figure made no attempt to move out of the way, so Cutajar braked to avoid him, but as he did so his car skidded on the wet road and plunged straight into the man – and out the other side! The man was no more substantial than a cloud and just

> vanished. Cutajar's car crashed into the grass verge, but happily he was uninjured. As for his "victim", it turns out that this is just one of several similar incidents reported from this stretch of road, seemingly haunted by the ghost of a man from an earlier century with no knowledge of modern traffic!

While the behaviour of the ghost in this story can be accounted for by his lack of knowledge of modern traffic laws, Linda Godfrey's story of the phantom jogger cannot. In *Weird Wisconsin,* we learn that Boltonville, Wisconsin's Jay Road, also known as Seven Bridges Road, has a persistent spirit that seems to be trapped in a cycle of reliving its death.

As Godfrey tells it:

> Along one particularly treacherous stretch [of the road] a young female jogger was struck and killed by an out-of-control car. Her body was never recovered from the swamp along the road. Years later, people still report encounters with the tormented jogger's ghost. They see a young woman in a jogging suit suddenly emerge from a mist in front of their car, inevitably too late to avoid her. After getting hit, the woman either disappears entirely or momentarily appears within the person's car to further torment them ...

It is a wonder that there haven't been more deaths along that stretch of road with that sort of horrible jump scare happening to unsuspecting drivers. Such an incident is enough to cause someone heart failure.

We can see why these phantom road accidents might occur – a traumatic emotional event seems to be able to leave an imprint behind that some people can see – but it interests me that, in both cases, the incident is associated with mist. It makes one wonder if the mist is not the Materia on which these recordings play or if a fog is not the place from which the recording materializes.

Phantom accidents are not the only fog-borne phantom events that occur in the paranormal world.

Loren Coleman, in *Curious Encounters*, gives the account of something curious that happened in Edwardsville, Kansas. J. F. Timmons had hired some workmen for his farm, and as all seemed well, he left them to get on with their work. The weather soon deteriorated though, and judging from the storm clouds and wind forming, the group decided they had better move to safer ground.

The work was happening adjacent to Kansas Pacific Railroad tracks, and the men had access to a handcar, which they got on the tracks and started posthaste for town. The group had only made a short distance when they saw what they thought was an oncoming locomotive. They, of course, scrambled to remove the handcar from the rails and then discovered that what they were seeing was not a train.

"Whatever it was came down the track giving off a volume of dense smoke with occasional flashes resembling a headlight at the centre of the smoke". This mystery object, which some UFO researchers would like to grab for their field, travelled three-quarters of a mile down the track, then veered off the track, circled a pile of cordwood, and moved off in a southwesterly direction, moving into thick forest.

I suppose this could have been a UFO in the style of the light anomalies that are sometimes seen in woodland, in among trees and closer to the ground than a typical UFO, but I have never heard of such an anomaly appearing in a curtain of smoke. I think we need to mark this one down as unknown and possibly a phantom train.

A more definite sighting of a phantom train is given in Brad Steiger's *Strange Disappearances.* Thomas Phillips was on a business trip on 10 January 1960 when he stopped for a train between Belleville and Sealy, Texas. He had spotted the train, which appeared to move from "a cloud of fog" about three hundred feet to his right.

Phillips had places to be, and as he waited impatiently for the train to pass, he noticed "that there were no crossing lights, signs, or signals". As the witness watched the train cars pass slowly by, he also said that the train seem to be illuminated "by a source entirely apart from the lights of [his] car".

When the train finally completed its transit, Phillips was surprised to see "that there was no sign of a railroad bed, not even a break in the pavement where one ever had been."

Steiger notes wryly that,"apparently, trains, too, can become lost in Space and Time". I think this well-known purveyor of the highly strange might have been more correct than he knew when this book was written in 1972.

Anyone with even a passing knowledge of ghost lore has heard of ghost or phantom ships such as the *Flying Dutchman.* In one of the books that turned me to the Charles Fort side in my youth, *Strange World*, Frank Edwards tells us of the old US Navy destroyer *Kennison* and mysterious events found in its logbook.

In early winter 1942, the *Kennison* was on patrol in San Francisco Bay, looking for Japanese submarines. The fog, which had formed suddenly, was so dense that visibility was poor, and the destroyer was edging its way along, relying on lookouts and the primitive radar of the time.

The lookout on the fantail, the rear or aft deck of a ship, called on the intercom for others to look to the rear of the ship. He also alerted the bridge as both he and the lookout on the after-gun deck stated that the *Kennison* "had been narrowly missed by what appeared to be a derelict two-masted sailing vessel which had plowed across within a few yards of the destroyer's stern". The "shabby, unmanned sailing vessel" had been in sight for about twenty-seconds and both lookouts had seen it, but there had been no contact from the ship's radar.

There is no follow-up to the *Kennison* story, but Brad Steiger gives us another ghost ship story in *Beyond Belief.* Here, too, we have another ghost ship "looming up out of the mist", and there is an interesting postscript to the story.

The event happened in April of 1936, and the observers were on board the SS *Khosrou.* The freighter was running a route between Calcutta and Bombay, and the weather had been execrable during most of the trip. On the day of the experience, the ship was making barely five knots in a "torrential downpour", and the captain had ordered the sounding of the siren every two minutes as a safety measure.

One of a sailor's worst nightmares is a collision with another ship in weather that would hamper rescue operations, so the sailors of the *Khosrou* tensed when they heard another siren sound, echoing that of their own ship. Power was cut to the engines, and the *Khosrou* coasted, blasting its siren, and being matched by the unknown ship. Eventually, the unknown vessel was sighted on the left side of the *Khosrou.*

The other ship was estimated at about six thousand tons and passed approximately 184 to 240 yards from the *Khosrou,* too close in that poor visibility. As she glided out of the mist and passed them, the sailors of the *Khosrou* were able to read her name on the side of the ship: *Tricouleur.*

The passing vessel seemed to be deserted, with an empty deck and no helmsman apparent at the wheel. The *Tricouleur* was visible to the officers and crew of the *Khosrou* before she glided back into the mist and rain.

Strangely, a very short time later, the weather let up and

visibility improved so that the men of the *Khosrou* could see for an estimated seven miles.

The *Tricouleur* was nowhere to be seen. Given the speed of the *Khosrou* and the fact that the two ships had passed ten minutes earlier, the *Tricouleur* should have been within three miles of the *Khosrou* and plainly visible. The mystery deepened when the navigator called the officers of the *Khosrou* into the chartroom.

"Just behind our position," the navigator stated, "about two miles back, there is a symbol labeling the spot of a wreck. Alongside the symbol you can see the notation: 'MS *Tricouleur,* with a cargo of chemicals, exploded and sank at this point at 5 p.m., on January 5, 1931'."

Steiger finishes this story with the note that it was six years to the hour since the phantom ship had gone down. The date of the sighting was 5 January 1937, and the time was 5:15 p.m.

For anyone who has spent time on the sea, this story tends to raise the hair on the back of the neck in its superb creepiness, but it is not simply trains and ships that have a phantom aspect.

Scott Harper, writing a witness account for *Phantoms and Monsters,* tells of a visit to his grandparents during his childhood that took a turn toward the bizarre.

Harper's grandfather was away, and as dense fog settled over the area, his grandmother seemed to become increasingly nervous. The location was a farmhouse in Central Ohio, and for some reason the seven-year-old could not understand, his grandmother did not want him looking out the window. Being a curious lad, he, of course, availed himself of the first opportunity he could find to peek outside.

The fog had been increasing in density, and the sun was setting, so darkness was imminent. Harper stared, fascinated, even though the visibility was poor, and wondered why his grandmother had suddenly become so opposed to him looking out the window. He found out soon enough:

> When the glow appeared in the fog, I had no idea what I was seeing, thinking the source, at first, to be car headlights. I stared harder, not quite believing my eyes, upon realizing that headlights weren't the answer. Gradually, the glow intensified, and I realized that the source of the glow was approaching my grandparents' house, moving along the road. The glow could soon be seen to actually be two glows – one yellow, the other pink. Both colors were washed-out, pastel shades.
>
> I kept watching, getting nervous. My jaw dropped a few moments later when the glows brightened, and their source came into view through the fog – two cows, dancing on their hind legs. One glowed pastel yellow, one glowed pastel pink. Each had a foreleg over the shoulder of the other, swaying, and dancing – almost staggering – their way along the road.

I admit that this account almost made me laugh out loud, but Harper's grandmother, who caught him at the window, took the event quite seriously. So seriously, in fact, that upon seeing the dancing cows, she promptly fainted.

When Harper's grandfather returned, the boy told him everything despite his grandmother's rejoinder to say nothing (presumably once she had regained consciousness). The older man went out to search the property with his rifle in hand but supposedly found nothing, though Harper says that he seemed agitated when he returned. Neither grandparent would discuss the event afterward.

I would love to conjecture on what the young Harper might have seen, but I honestly have no idea what would produce the apparition of dancing, pastel-glowing cows. Given the grandparents' reaction, one wonders if the dense fog in that area had produced other, less whimsical apparitions or creatures in the past.

The elders certainly seemed determined not to speak of the experience ever again, and it is true that in certain belief sets to speak of something summons it or gives it power. Perhaps the grandparents were having some trickster-type experiences on the farm and did not want to encourage their harasser?

We've seen phantom accidents, smoke-cloaked balls of light on railroad tracks, phantom trains, phantom ships and even phantom cows in the mist. Now, we turn briefly to another paranormal phenomenon that has a reputation for vanishing into mist or appearing to be wrapped in the stuff.

SHADOW PEOPLE

Veteran researcher of the strange Rosemary Ellen Guiley speaks of the so-called Shadow People or Shadow Men in her book *The Djinn Connection.* In the book, it seems to me that Guiley was trying to use the djinn as a sort of unified field theory of the paranormal. While I disagree with this hypothesis, based on my own experience, I have a lot of respect for this late seeker of the truth and wanted to include a couple of stories from the aforementioned book here.

Guiley had her own experience when she was twelve and sleeping over at a friend's house. The two girls were sleeping on mattresses on the floor in the friend's bedroom. Suddenly, the pair experienced feelings of extreme fear and the familiar sense of being watched. Both sat up in the makeshift beds and "saw a hooded/cloaked shadow standing in the doorway. It had slanted, glowing red eyes that seemed to be staring at me. It [the figure] was completely dark and it did not seem to have a definite shape. I would describe it as 'shrouded in darkness', like it had a light mist surrounding it ..."

Guiley states that it was the glowing eyes that held her attention and that the rest of the figure seemed to appear only in her peripheral vision. She also noted that she felt as though she could not look away from the being, as if all she could do was stare at the thing, and she seems to have felt some lapse in her memory. Her friend told her later that the experience had lasted about ten-seconds and that the Shadow Person simply disappeared after that.

The sleepover friend frankly admitted that the being had "scared her to bits", and neither she nor Guiley were willing to discuss the event for several days afterward. I often wonder if this unwillingness to talk about an incident of high strangeness and the often-unreasoning terror that accompanies the event is not a side effect of being in the presence of one of these beings whether it is a Shadow Person, a Phantom Black Dog or a Sasquatch. I'll have more to say about this in the conclusion.

Ms. Guiley was also well known, later in life, for her work with psychic development. I've known any number of natural psychics throughout my life, and they seem to attract weirdness until they get better control of their abilities. I have to wonder if this late and lamented researcher wasn't, even then, beginning to evidence some psychic talent that attracted this apparition.

Jason Offutt has written about the Shadow People in his book *Darkness Walks* and tells the story of Dawn Sevier of Sparta, Tennessee. Sevier had experienced Shadow People on several occasions, but her worst experience happened after a "bad experience in the hospital". During recovery from surgery, Sevier had a bad reaction to medication that produced an out-of-body experience (OOBE).

No one can really define an OOBE, but for practical purposes, let's say that the experiencer has a distinct sense of having some part of themselves separate from the physical body. In many stress-related OOBEs, that separate part stays close to the physical body, but there are techniques for inducing an OOBE and then travelling. These journeys can remain in our physical plane or, seemingly, explore another world.

In any event, the witness was staying with a friend as she healed, and on the first night, she again experienced an OOBE, perhaps as the result of being "heavily medicated" (for some, sedation tends to loosen the connection between the physical and that part that journeys out of the physical). As the woman stood looking at her physical body, she had the sense that something was standing to her left (presumably the left of her astral form) but could not turn to see what it was. Since she could not turn left, she looked right and found "the wall ... vibrating faster and faster."

A Shadow Person appeared through the wall with a form that seemed to be made of black oil. Sevier notes that the body seemed muscular, the eyes were almond-shaped and black and red, and the being did not appear to have any hair. Peculiarly, this Shadow Person had "red blood veins, like humans have blue ones, running all through its muscular structure ... it stood about seven feet tall, and it couldn't see me at all."

What the being did seem attracted to was the physical body that Sevier was not completely occupying at the time. As she noticed this and prepared to fight the thing for her physical body, she realized that the being had no feet – instead, its "legs faded to black-and-red mist". Sevier saw this and was seized with the urge to jump back into her unconscious body.

As she had this thought, the Shadow Person dissolved into a cloud of black and red mist, which began to wrap itself around Sevier's sleeping form. The witness seems to have been successful in re-entering her body as "... Suddenly I found myself throwing covers off myself and screaming 'no' ... I demanded that the thing leave me alone, I told it that it couldn't touch me ..."

Interestingly, though the witness awakened soaked with

sweat, she recounts that she was not afraid but instead felt angry that the being had tried to "invade [her] space".

While this witness was having an OOBE and many people might discard her report as nothing more than the misfiring of her drug-addled brain, one has only to look at the impressive literature to discover that Sevier's experience was entirely congruent with other OOBE experiencers. This includes the experience of having entities harass them while they are out of body, and in fact, we will discuss such an experience by the author Robert Bruce in another section.

I think that we disregard testimony from those who are not seated in their bodies at our own risk. OOBEs may be what they seem to be, an exit of a part of the person from their physical shell, or they may be a form of vivid, traveling clairvoyance. In either case, they can reveal astoundingly accurate facts about our consensual reality and produce intriguing information about other realms.

In another Shadow Person story from Offutt, we encounter Mikk, who had an experience where the being actually drove him out of his body.

The seventeen-year-old lived in North York, Toronto, and was sleeping soundly in his bedroom on that night in 1977. He was wakened from sleep by something that felt like a "sharp kick in the ribs". The youth lay still, gasping for air and unable to call for help, convinced that an intruder had hit him with a hockey stick (a common accoutrement in a Canadian household) and hidden in his closet.

The witness was watching the closet door when "heavy smoke blew into [his] room then drew together into a human shape". The being took a hooded, monk-like form that reminded Mikk of the popular version of Death. Mikk's vision of this thing had no legs. The being prodded him several times, saying, "questions, questions" repeatedly. Mikk had no idea how to respond.

The being seemed to be two dimensional. When it turned from Mikk, it seemed to be no more than a "pencil mark". Apparently tiring of the question game, the entity extended a finger into Mikk's mind and seemed to feed off of all his negative emotions, filing through his memories for examples of lust or avarice or hatred. Mikk felt certain that the being was going to suck the life force out of him.

Once this terrible memory download was complete, the Death figure leapt on Mikk and, according to the young man, drove him out of his body and into "the other side". The Shadow Person invited him to stay there, and when Mikk refused, the entity unexpectedly let the youth go. He felt himself returning to his body, and when he came to full consciousness, the being was gone.

Mikk returned to sleep and commented that, in the morning, "the sunshine never looked so great".

After having a parasite suck your life force and interfere with your memories, I imagine that truer words were never spoken. One might be inclined to pass this experience off as a vivid dream except that it aligns with so many other Shadow Person experiences.

If one person tells you something, it may or may not be objectively true, but when a mass of witnesses testifies to very similar phenomena, then I think we need to pay attention. Even if these experiences don't occur in the consensual reality, they do occur, and they can be every bit as traumatic as events in the "real world".

In his book *Ghostly Adventures*, Christopher Balzano tells the story of Beth and Stacey, two young women who rented an apartment together in a tough neighbourhood of Dallas, Texas. Stacey apparently had some metaphysical awareness, as she placed crystals at the front and back entrances to the apartment as protective talismans. Crystals, especially pure quartz, are simple to cleanse of disharmonic energies and then program with a specific intention, and they are a common part of New Age and magical households.

Beth, not really understanding what the crystals were for, moved one of them while cleaning and failed to replace it.

Immediately, the atmosphere of the apartment changed. Friends would come to visit and leave quickly, commenting that they needed air. Two days after the crystal was moved, the pair were settling for bed when Beth noticed a black shadow behind the television in the room. "The object was as tall as the ceiling and four feet wide". Stacey soon asked Beth if she could see the thing, which appeared "more like thick, black smoke than a shadow. There was no sound coming from it, and it did not give off an odor ..."

Both young women agreed that the figure was negative and that it gave off a feeling of anger and bad feelings. Stacey gathered the courage to run and turn on the lights, but this failed to affect the being, so the two called Stacey's cousin, Brandy, a psychic with experience of the paranormal. The roommate watched, as they waited, as the "streams of smoke that made [the entity] up moved like a lava lamp and then bled into one another ..."

The cousin, Brandy, finally appeared, and the young women rushed to let her in, but despite Brandy's best efforts, the Shadow Person refused to be moved and, in fact, seemed to be affecting Stacey, causing her to "fade out" and then "complain about a stabbing pain in her back". Eventually, the cloud simply faded away and disappeared, but neither of the two roommates felt that it really left.

After a string of misfortunes involving both their love lives and their employment, the two young women decided to pack up and move. Though they had subsequent ghost experiences, neither of them ever experienced anything like this again.

No one has, or I think can, settle what the Shadow People are. Rosemary Ellen Guiley was convinced that they were yet another form of the djinn, and there could be some merit to this argument. Others have posited that they are some sort of inter-dimensional being or even demons.

As I outlined in *Phantom Black Dogs,* the use of the word demon to connote any sort of hostile spirit is a misnomer. I cite occultist Michelle Belanger in defining what, exactly, a demon is:

> The being must be non-human (in other words, not simply a nasty ghost), with a malevolent agenda aimed at living human beings. Additionally, the being must be self-aware and intelligent. It will be aware of the people it is victimizing and often seems to have a certain glee and harsh intent in its malice ...

Finally, Belanger states that a demon will have a certain intuitive feel that assists in discerning it from other spirits, ghosts, etc. I would add that the demon, as opposed to any other type of Otherworld entity, clearly seems to have an interest in obsessing and/or possessing human beings. (Author's note: the demon has also never had a physical body of its own.)

While some of the Shadow People accounts above could certainly be demonic in origin, Mikk's story for example, we also have to remember a concept that I introduced earlier: the ecosphere of spirits has as many, if not more, spiritual beings as the ecosphere of this planet. Some of those spirits tolerate humans more than others, and we do not need to jump to demons to explain every hostile spirit incursion.

We have discussed several kinds of spirits and phantoms in the above pages. Now, we will move on to one of the most puzzling enigmas of the modern age: UFOs. These seeming vehicles and their occupants have a long association with fog, mist, and smoke.

SECTION THREE

UFOS AND RELATED PHENOMENA

UFOS, PART I

As I noted in *Phantom Black Dogs*, I realize that the new "hip" initials for flying anomalies are UAP (unidentified aerial phenomena), but I will refer to them throughout this section as UFOs (unidentified flying objects). I grew up in the era of "flying saucers", and some of my earliest explorations of the strange were in books on UFOs. It is a thought habit I find hard to break.

When we dive into the UFO end of the pool, we get immediately into deep waters. There is nothing standard about UFOs other than the fact that people are seeing unexplainable things in the sky and that those things do sometimes fall into broad categories. What was interesting to me, in doing the research for this book, was the frequency with which smoke and mists are associated with these unknown phenomena.

While I live in Canada, I'm originally from Texas. I grew up with a father who, after his UFO sighting in California in the 1950s, firmly believed that there was a UFO base in the Hill Country, outside San Antonio. I'm not so sure about that, but I do know that Texas is home to a couple of sets of the UFO subset known as a ghost lights.

Most famous of these ghost lights are the so-called Marfa Lights. Marfa is way out in West Texas, but there is another, lesser known, set of ghost lights in the area called the Big Thicket, on the other side of the state in East Texas. The Thicket, as you can imagine, is an area of dense forest that is also well known for sightings of a Sasquatch-like creature and is not too far from the swamp homeland of the Louisiana Rougarou.

In the Big Thicket, one might also see the Big Thicket Ghost Light, also known as the Bragg Light, since it is often seen in "the vicinity of Bragg Road near Saratoga". Interestingly, while the light often appears as a luminous "bush-white sphere the size of a basketball", it is also sometimes seen as "a vaguely defined bright spot in what appears to be a small luminous fog bank".

Unlike the Marfa Lights, which can be viewed from miles away across the desert, the Bragg Light is limited to open areas in the Big Thicket, and witnesses are often closer to the phenomenon than those who see the Marfa Lights. Given what we have already seen about strange fog banks and what we will learn later, I would advise anyone encountering one of the these "small luminous fog banks" to keep their distance.

Linda Godfrey, in *I Know What I Saw*, relates a UFO story from the beginning of the modern UFO age. The *Hillsboro-Sentry-Enterprise* headline for 26 February 1948 read "Flying 'Fence Posts' Seen Near Hillsboro". It seems that two unrelated witnesses saw the UFOs at about 1130 hours that morning. The witnesses heard a "mechanical roaring" above them, and since the town was not subject to air traffic, they were surprised enough by the sound to look up. What they saw was something that they could not identify as an aircraft of the time: "two white, horizontal objects that resembled giant white fence posts roaring through the air in precise alignment ..."

One witness, a farmer named Sidney Shear, reported that "each was a long tapering cylinder with a slightly bulbous head and fan tail of light-colored gas or mist". The UFOs slowed as the witnesses watched, and turned on their ends, so that they stood up vertically, then made their slow way to the horizon. The witnesses said that the objects were quite large, and Godfrey conjectures that they were each about eighty feet long.

If the objects had remained in a more horizontal alignment and stayed at a constant speed, one might surmise that the witnesses had seen the test of a rocket or missile. Neither of these things is the case, however, and the vertical orientation of the UFOs and the variation in their speed speak to something more mysterious than human technology.

There is no indication that the "fan tail of light-colored gas or mist" had anything to do with the objects' propulsion, especially given the orientation of these objects on a vertical axis while they continued to move toward the horizon. As we'll see, these mists are seen in UFO sightings throughout time, but they have varying effects.

A couple of famous UFO incidents occurred in 1952, and both have mysterious mists to deal with.

One of the cases is shrouded in controversy. Witness "Sonny" Desvergers had an alleged sighting on 19 August 1952 while he was driving three Boy Scouts home. Reportedly, the man saw a "strange light" off in the palmettos and stopped his car to go investigate. He noticed an odd scent and came upon a "a large, oval object hovering 30 feet above a clearing".

Of interest to us, this UFO emitted a red mist that enveloped the witness, who then lost consciousness. When he came to, Desvergers "fled the scene, running into the scouts further down the road".

The witness was familiar with acids that were used in his workplace but could not place the smell of the mist that had allegedly knocked him out. This case has been rumoured to be a hoax, and Desvergers' account has changed over time. Still, the basic form of the tale does coincide with other accounts, so I decided to include it here.

The other 1952 event that Cutchin relates to us is the famous Flatwoods Monster case, which has been the subject of books and an excellent documentary from *Small Town Monsters.* The basic shape of the story is that, on 12 September 1952, two young brothers and their friend saw a bright object cross the West Virginia sky at about 1915 hours. This object disappeared on land adjacent to where the boys lived, and they gathered up a party of people, including their mother, a National Guardsman and two adult friends to see what the object might be.

As they approached the neighbour's property, the family dog bolted ahead and then returned shortly with its tail tucked. The seven witnesses walked up a hill and found what looked like a fifty-foot fireball pulsing in the forest. As the group got closer, a "noxious mist" rolled out of the tree line, producing an irritant effect on their eyes and noses.

This mist often gets forgotten since, at this point, the monster appears from the woods as well: a ten-foot-tall figure with a spade-shaped head and a body covered in "a skirt of green armor". Thoroughly terrified, the group fled, "coughing and screaming all the way".

The excitement was not over for the evening. Two other witnesses, travelling from Queens, New York, to Cincinnati, Ohio, were travelling through Braxton County when their vehicle simply stopped. The driver got out of the car and immediately smelt "ether and burnt sulfur" right before the woodland began to glow and a being similar to the one seen in the early encounter appeared. The driver returned to the vehicle as quickly as he could, and the entity dragged a hand across the windshield. Once the monster was out of sight, the witnesses were able to start the car and drive on toward their destination and away from whatever haunted the forests of Flatwoods.

Whatever the mist was, it had a deleterious effect on the witnesses, including the dog mentioned earlier, which died. The human witnesses all experienced running eyes and noses as well as vomiting hours after their contact with the being. Given Desvergers' experience and the effect on the Flatwoods witnesses, one might wonder if whatever these people encountered was simply trying to defend itself.

Whether UFOs are structured craft piloted by extraterrestrials or some other type of interdimensional phenomena, any being that studies human beings for more than fifteen minutes will know that we are a violent species. Knowing this, the UFOs could have defence mechanisms, such as these mists, to keep people away from them or put them in a condition where they cannot do harm.

Linda Godfrey, in *American Monsters*, reports that the occupants of a craft that landed on a road in Playa Del Rey, California, were much more innocuous. Three drivers in three different vehicles were forced to stop when their cars ceased to work in the presence of this object on 6 November 1957. The drivers all testified that the UFO was egg-shaped and "partly obscured by bluish mist" and that the occupants of the egg had "yellowish green skin" and wore "black leather pants, white belts and light-colored jerseys".

These strange chartreuse occupants tried to interrogate the witnesses, but none of the drivers could understand them. We aren't really told what happened after this attempted conversation, but one assumes the occupants mounted up and left the same way that they had arrived. Godfrey notes that the local constabulary received a number of reports of UFOs for the same day and area.

As with the flying fence post case above, this mist seems to simply be related to the UFO and did not produce any noxious effects. It is possible the mist was some sort of by-product of functions on the craft, or perhaps the occupants did not feel threatened by the witnesses or were of a milder nature than the Flatwoods being.

There is a theory that some UFOs are the result of what researchers call earth lights, a phenomenon associated with strain on the tectonic plates of the earth. In *Borderlands,* Mike Dash gives a classic example of how earth lights might work, and as you might imagine, mists are involved in this witness testimony.

In the Welsh town of Bridgend, somewhere in the mid 1960s, "a couple were standing in their back garden when they heard a noise like that of a distant jet engine and saw a white patch of sparkling mist appear low on the horizon". As the couple watched:

> ... a reddish light materialized by the side of the mist, joined up with it and then started to blink. The mist then began to glow and pulsate, dividing into two sections. These sections began to spin round and around. The smaller of the two now moved on top of the larger one, giving the overall impression of an object looking like a squashed bowler hat. Lights of many colours now came on the bottom of the object, which now began to solidify into a metallic-looking disc shape with a dome on top, broken only by a reddish glow underneath ...

The object continued to move about for a few minutes, and the strange sound came back before the object took on a more mistlike appearance again and then disappeared.

Now, honestly, I don't know if this had anything at all to do with tectonic strain, but it certainly seems a fine example of a UFO forming out of mist. One wonders if the mists seen with the "flying fence posts" and the egg-shaped UFO of Playa del Rey weren't simply after-products of the formation of these unusual sights.

The classic volume *Dimensions*, by Jacques Vallee, returns us to mists that are used for defensive or, in this case, almost offensive purposes.

On 4 September 1964, Mr. S was hunting in the mountains of Northern California. The man lost track of his party and, with night falling, lit some fires so that searchers might more easily find him. As he settled in to wait, the man noted a light in the sky that he hoped was the light of a searching helicopter. Unfortunately for Mr. S, the light came to a completely silent hover nearby. Recognizing that the object was unusual, he climbed a tree to have a better look.

After the witness "saw a flash and a dark object fell to the ground", the hunter saw two figures approaching from the woods. Both were short, a little over five feet tall, and had on silver uniforms that covered their heads. A third entity appeared later, which seemed more robot-like, darker with "two reddish-orange eyes".

These beings tried to lure Mr. S out of the tree, but he managed to keep them away by throwing bits of flaming paper and clothing at them. The "robot-like" being dropped its lower jaw, then placed its "hand" inside a "cavity thus revealed", causing it to emit "a puff of smoke" in the hunter's direction.

"The smoke spread like a mist and, upon reaching him, made him lose consciousness". The hunter later compared exposure to this stuff with being deprived of oxygen.

So, apparently, when these beings, whatever they are, want to visit with you, it is difficult to avoid them. Given Vallee's and others' opinion that UFO occupants might be related to the folkloric faery (see *Passport to Magonia),* I have to wonder what would have happened if Mr. S had been in possession of a size-able chunk of "cold iron"?

We've only just reached the 1960s, so there is more UFO and mist lore in the next chapter.

UFOS, PART 2

One of the things that I began to wonder, as I dug deeply into the subject of this text, was how many of the clouds, mists, and fogs that we see on a daily basis are actually hiding something mysterious.

In the book *Unexplained*, Jerome Clark gives a terrific example of this "object hiding in plain sight" scenario. The witness, a "tourist", was gazing out the window of "a clifftop home along the seashore at Sydney, Australia". The incident happened in the spring of 1965 in the late afternoon and began with the tourist taking note of an attractive pink cloud that was not moving.

An hour elapsed, and when she looked again, the pink cloud was approaching the witness. The mystery cloud was soon actually below the witness' eye level, and she could see that there was a "round, white object" embedded in it and that, in fact, the cloud seemed to be produced from vents in the side of this craft.

The artificial creation of a cloud as cover is quite amazing enough, but the witness then testifies that a ladder was lowered from the bottom of the object, and a "human-like figure" descended to sit on the beach. The figure shone what looked like a searchlight out to sea and seemed to be answered by a pink flare off in the ocean.

The creature jumped back into its craft, and the UFO shot off toward the flare. The tourist then noted a "long but not clearly visible shape in the water from which the flare had ascended". Both the white object that had produced the cloud and whatever was under the water vanished in a "vivid pink flash".

These sorts of incidents always seem to me to set the extraterrestrial hypothesis on its ear. Why would an entity with the technology to come to Earth from a distant star need a ladder to climb down to the seashore? Why would this scion of advanced technology not be able to find the object that it rendezvoused with at sea, and on the same point, why would it need to use a searchlight and flares for location purposes?

Surely, if one can navigate interstellar space, one ought to be able to find one's buddies under the sea. This is just one of many reasons why I think there is far more to the UFO phenomenon than space people rocketing around in ships.

Jerome Clark has another UFO cloud story in *Unexplained.*

Two Finnish skiers had an experience similar to the Australian tourist on 7 January 1970. As they indulged in their hobby, they "encountered a mysterious luminous red cloud". When it got closer to them, the two testified that this cloud, too, contained a domed disc that was actually producing the smoke.

As with the Aussie case, the UFO cast enough light for the skiers to see a "three-foot-tall humanoid with a waxy, pale face on the ground just under the UFO". Interestingly, the red cloud reappeared quickly, as though the occupant realized it was being observed, and, by the time the cloud had faded away, both the UFO and its presumed occupant were gone.

At least this small person was not having trouble locating others of its kind, but again we see the craft seeming to produce this smoke. At this point in the proceedings, one begins to wonder if the smoke is camouflage so that these craft, whatever they are, can move about mostly unobserved or if the smoke is a sign of something more mysterious happening.

1970 was not too late for the beginning of a contactee event, and the incident in Imjarvi, Finland, is well known amongst UFO researchers. Lon Strickler, in *Phantoms and Monsters*, gives the details of the contactees' first contact.

This is an example of another set of skiers being caught out by a UFO. Aarno Heinonen and Esko Viljo spotted a "10-foot-wide metallic object with a flat bottom, wrapped at first in a reddish gray mist" after noting a buzzing sound in their area. The craft came down to a height of ten to twelve feet above them (Heinonen stated that he could have touched it with his ski pole), and a light beam descended from the bottom of the UFO. The beam, oddly, illuminated an area with a diameter of about three feet, but the edges of the illumination were black.

The red-grey mist came down, and when it dissipated, the pair saw a "three-foot-tall humanoid creature" standing in the beam of light, holding a "black box with a pulsating yellow light". This being was about ten feet from the two men and was described with thin arms and legs, a waxy face with a hooked nose, and wearing coveralls, boots, gauntlets and a "conical metallic helmet". I can't help visualizing a sort of goblin from this description.

Once more, the reddish grey mist descended, and sparks seemed to emanate from the lighted area where the being had stood. The witnesses stated that a "sort of flame arose from this spot and entered the UFO. The mist dissipated, and the UFO vanished along with it.

It's interesting to note that, as with the witnesses to the

Flatwoods Monster who inhaled the noxious vapours, these two men also suffered physiological effects, including vomiting, leg numbness and passing black urine. Two years later, Heinonen claimed to experience "a series of contacts with a female spacewoman".

Again, we see a mist of fog either serving as obscuration so that the occupant and vessel in the story can move unnoticed or as a vehicle for something that resembles teleportation. Also, given the neurological effects noted repeatedly with exposure to the mists and clouds around UFOs, one wonders what contribution the smoke exposure in this case had to the contact experiences later. This incident gives one the impression that the two witnesses were being "primed" for later events.

Our witnesses, to this point in the chapter, seem not to have been too terrified by their encounters, but when we move to Brazil for a witness encounter in 1971, we see a completely different scenario. The witness in this case was so afraid of the UFO he encountered that he performed an almost superhuman feat as he fled the craft.

In his book *UFO Danger Zone*, Bob Pratt relates the tale of a young man walking home from work in the dark on 22 March 1971 at about 2330 hours. He saw something in the bushes, which he at first mistook for a big head with red eyes but then realized was a glowing ball of light. This fellow, named Jose, didn't try to hide or hunker down and see what would happen. He ran for all he was worth. Even a brief perusal of UFO lore in Brazil will reveal that UFOs in that country have a deadlier reputation than they do in other parts of the world, with a number of injuries and fatalities attributed to the mysterious craft.

Jose had to clear about four hundred yards to make it to his home, and a hundred of those yards took him over a dam, which had a safety rail on the water side but nothing to prevent a fifty-foot drop to rocks below on the other side. Investigators who crossed the dam in broad daylight testified that they were nervous making their way across the structure at a walk. Jose cleared the dam at a flat-out run in the middle of the night, so great was his terror.

When I got to the dam, the object came very close to me. It was about ten meters [about 32 feet] in diameter and had blue, pink and red colors on it. The light was about as bright as a fifteen-watt bulb and was giving out smoke and vapor. It came down very low over the water [behind the dam]. I thought they were trying to catch me ...

Jose did make it back to his house, unlike some of his fellow countrymen, and his mother let the panicked man back into the home. Given what we have seen about some of the mists associated with UFOs, I suspect that Jose did well to avoid breathing any of the vapour coming off that object.

In a less fear-filled sighting in 1977, Dr. Francisco Padron Leon of the Canary Islands was riding in a taxi, on his way to see a patient, when he had his encounter. Chris O'Brien tells us in *Stalking the Herd* that both the doctor and his driver saw an enormous glowing blue sphere, approximately one hundred feet in diameter, hovering near the ground in front of the car.

Leon later testified that he could see "stars in the night sky" through the object and that there appeared to be two beings in the craft, working at a console. Abruptly, the sphere filled with "bluish smoke", which seemed to make the sphere enlarge to an even greater diameter before rising into the air and flying off toward Tenerife.

In some of our cases, the smoke or fog or mist seems to be a transport or camouflage medium. In this case, the smoke not only hides the occupants of this sphere from view but also alters the size of the craft. I was minded of the stories of Phantom Black Dogs where efforts to move the Dog from the path only made the creature larger so that it blocked more of the road.

Our final story for this chapter takes place on 7 May 1980 and introduces another common theme in UFO literature, the idea of missing time. This account comes to us from Jacques Vallee in his book *Confrontations* and is worth quoting at some length:

> Mrs. Anderson had just picked up Janet [her daughter] at her karate class. It was 9:05 p.m. They were driving south, approaching the bridge over the Sacramento River [in Redding California], when they saw a luminous cloud "explode" and engulf the car. All sound stopped. Mrs. Anderson said they seemed to be "floating along". When they emerged from the cloud, they looked back but could see no trace of it behind the car. They stopped to buy some soft drinks and drove to their friend's house. It is at that point they noticed it was 10:10 p.m., over half an hour later than it "should have been" ...

Mrs. Anderson, who had worked at a nuclear research facility, described the cloud to me as an energized blast with a beam of light travelling at the top of it. It was glowing. She felt as if the flashing light "went through" her head with a painful sensation. It see[med] to her that, "time had stopped", but the feeling was not negative. In fact, Linda commented, "It's as if God had sent this cloud to us."

While the daughter Janet is mentioned in the quote above, it should be noted that Mrs. Anderson also had her daughter Connie in the vehicle at the time of the encounter.

Janet, riding in the back seat and crying, mourning a recent break-up with her boyfriend, looked up when her mother called out about the cloud. Janet found it odd that, when they exited the cloud, her tears had dried and everyone in the car was very thirsty.

Connie was riding in the front of the station wagon and remembered only seeing a pulsating light and the road becoming foggy before the car entered a bright cloud. "Everything became silent, super-slow, and creepy ..." Connie told Vallee later.

All the witnesses agreed that the weather was fair. The cloud, apparently, came out of nowhere.

I found this story fascinating since it has most of the elements of what researcher Jenny Randles calls the "Oz Effect". The silence that descended with the cloud and the feeling of timelessness are both signs of the Oz Effect at work, and the only signal missing was that this family seemed to be taken completely by surprise. Randles tells us that most percipients who have the Oz Effect have a feeling something is about to happen directly before the event.

A non-Oz related effect that I found interesting was the observation, made by Janet, that her tears had dried and that everyone in the car was thirsty when they exited the anomalous cloud. We have seen a number of physical effects from these clouds, but we will encounter other accounts where, for example, a very wet person becomes dry or a vehicle is warm to the touch after an incident.

In the meantime, however, we have one last set of UFO tales to peruse.

UFOS, PART 3

The story of the Andersons in the last chapter moved us into the 1980s, but we would be remiss if we did not look at one of the most famous UFO events of all time – the Rendlesham Forest Incident.

I am not even going to attempt to delve into the complexities of the Rendlesham event; the incident had so many moving parts that it has been the subject of books and documentaries attempting to detail the complex net of events. Suffice to say that, in late December of 1980, on two separate nights, servicemen at RAF Woodbridge, which was then being used by the United States Air Force, witnessed anomalous lights and even a structured craft in the vicinity of the base.

One thing to understand about Rendlesham is that part of the problem in summarizing the case is the sheer number of witnesses and the apparent dissimulation of command personnel after the event. Service members who responded to either lights or, at one point, what they thought might be a downed aircraft, divided into groups, each composed of multiple personnel. Thus, we have a variety of accounts, from many different perspectives, to choose from in examining this case.

In *Strange but True,* well-known British ufologist Jenny Randles tells us that while Deputy Base Commander Lieutenant Colonel Charles Halt was observing a large, airborne object moving over a field towards the coast, which subsequently seemed to explode, break into pieces and vanish, there was activity elsewhere in the wood. Airmen in another area saw a flash of light, which preceded the appearance of a "ghostly car-sized object sitting on the ground and riding on a cushion of yellowish mist".

After this event, and others of the night of 26 December, a team of USAF personnel returned to the putative landing site near the eastern edge of the forest and found a tripod-like impression on the ground as well as scorch marks and broken tree branches. There is some question about the ufological basis for this evidence.

What we do know is that the deputy base commander led a group of servicemen into the woods during the early morning hours of 28 December and that his audio-recorded notes from the mission are still extant. In addition to finding levels of radiation at the landing site higher than base radiation in the area, a smaller group, walking through the forest, encountered a "dancing red light inside an eerily pulsating fog". The service members who spotted this craft stated that it was "metal and conical, with a bright red light above and a circle of blue lights below, and suspended in a yellow mist".

As I noted, Rendlesham is a well-known topic amongst UFO researchers, and there are books on the subject, but I find it fascinating that even in this most-viewed UFO report, we have the mention of mysterious mists. I also see a pattern, after looking at the preceding UFO reports, of the mists associated with UFOs being coloured – pink, reddish grey, yellow, etc. I am not sure what the significance of this might be, but the colour of a mist or fog might be an indicator of the purpose for the visual obscuration.

Chris Holly, in her *Endless Journey* blog, gives the account of a young woman who, with her roommate, saw a UFO off the coast of San Diego, California, in 1980. The eighteen-year-old woman felt compelled to get into her car and go to the beach with her roommate, an illogical thing to do since the beach was an easy walk from their apartment. The beach was socked in with dense fog, so the two women parked the car and walked toward the water.

"Once they got about 20 feet from the shoreline the fog broke exposing a crystal-clear corridor that was approximately 150 yards wide by about one mile in length". Drawn by a humming noise, the roommates looked up to see an "iridescent looking craft" moving smoothly above their heads. The witnesses felt that they lost some time, and when next they were able to track the object, it was moving away and then vanished to sight.

There is no mention as to whether the fog dissipated or moved back in to fill up the mysterious clear space where the object appeared, but once again, we see fog or mist associated with a possible missing time interval.

In her book taken from the television show *Sightings*, Susan Michaels relates the hair-raising experience of the Knowles family, who were driving from Perth, Australia, to Melbourne, a distance of 1,600 miles. Faye Knowles and her sons – Sean, Patrick and Wayne – were taking the drive in shifts, trying to save money by not stopping for the night.

By 0230 hours, 21 January 1988, the family was deep into the Victorian Desert and stopped for gas and snacks at a station on the Nullarbor Plain. Sean was driving, unobstructed by traffic at the late hour, when he noted a yellow light ahead "in the middle of the road". The bright light turned out to be a luminous egg-shaped craft, which Sean had to swerve to avoid. At the same time, the young man woke his brother Patrick, telling him that he was seeing a UFO.

For a moment, it appeared that the Knowles would drive away from the incident, but then the UFO began to give chase. Patrick, thoroughly alarmed by the unknown craft's behaviour, urged his brother to pick up speed. At one point, the two witnesses estimate that they were driving almost 125 miles per hour but were unable to escape their pursuer.

Sean tried to shake the UFO by turning and heading in the other direction but to no avail, so he resumed their original course toward Melbourne. By this time, everyone in the car was awake, and the family dog had joined the chorus of concern.

A beam of light lanced out from the UFO, and one of the back tires of the car blew out. Sean fought for control and got the car stopped, but the UFO landed on the roof of the vehicle and "picked the car up". The witnesses describe the car being "lit up" like a "microwave", and they felt that they were being dehydrated as they sat. Wayne stated that he felt he was being pulled from his body.

Faye stuck her hand out the window and was seriously burned. Sean related that the car began to fill "with a thick, black fog. It was so hot, and all this soot, this junk, started covering us. Our voices started changing. You know how a tape deck sounds when the batteries go flat? That's what it was like. I think I blacked out."

The car continued to fill with the black fog and soot, which covered everything in the vehicle and smelled horrible, "like dead bodies". Abruptly though, there was a loud noise, and the car crashed back to earth. The Knowles family exited the vehicle and tried to hide from the UFO in the desert scrub. Oddly, the family matriarch says that when she turned off the car lights, the object no longer seemed able to track the car.

The UFO fled at dawn, but again, the family experienced time distortion. They assumed that the event had only lasted about fifteen minutes but discovered that the time elapsed had been an hour and a half.

I will note here the strange dehydrating effect that we saw in the Anderson case and will see in a later incident. Again, we have this odd circumstance where a seemingly high-tech craft suddenly loses a motor vehicle, something that our technology can track with ease, when the lights are turned off.

In another, less dramatic incident, Peter McCue tells us in *Britain's Paranormal Forests* of an incident that happened in the hotspot area of Cannock Chase, August 1988. A couple driving in the dark on a road that skirted the northern end of the Chase saw a "circular mass glowing with a deep reddish colour that pulsed. There was a surrounding cloud or mist, which touched the top of the hedge.

> "A semi-solid object" appeared to come forth from the mass; then the mass vanished, only to reappear farther north a short time later. The mass then vanished again, but the witnesses were left with a "strange sense of calm and sudden quietness".

There were signs of damage to the hedge on investigation, but I can't help thinking that this is one of the few events that we have looked at where the outcome was entirely positive. Jenny Randles, one of the investigators, thinks that this might have been an instance of "atmospheric plasma" or "earth lights" since the incident occurred on a "geologically faulted area". It's possible that electromagnetic fluctuation from the fault zone could have influenced the brains of the percipients, causing the feeling of well-being. It seems to me that before we can place this case in the explained file, we would need to know why the fault was under strain at this particular time.

Returning to the theme of UFOs moving cars, Australia is not the only place where this happens. In *Secrets of the Mysterious Valley,* Chris O'Brien tells of a witness who claimed to see multiple UFOs over his property. This individual even claimed that he and his mother had been able to call the craft closer using their minds. This witness told O'Brien the following interesting story:

> One night, toward the end of May, a friend (who didn't believe they had been seeing the craft) and I went out a couple miles north of the ranch to watch. It was around 9:00 to 9:30 p.m. We were sitting in his pickup truck, out in the middle of nowhere, when a strange bank of fog rolled in and surrounded us. We saw a light straight ahead shining out of the fog and a craft appeared and hovered in front of us, about two hundred yards away. I started to call it closer and it approached and just sat there about fifty feet away. Well, my friend kind of freaked out, grabbed his rifle from the rack and popped off a couple of shots at it. It went above us and somehow it lifted up the truck and put it in the bar ditch!

I found this report interesting not just because of the fog bank but also because of the reaction of the UFO to being fired on. Apparently, the occupants of these craft don't like being shot at any more than the Phantom Black Dogs in my first book! I suspect that these two witnesses were fortunate that the reaction of the Other was not stronger than it was.

As a final bit of UFO strangeness, I include this account from Andrew Nicholson's book *Weird Australia*.

In February 2009, the witness was out walking her dog about a local racetrack. She noticed a small man about two hundred metres in front of her and, when the man gave her a friendly wave, approached him and engaged him in conversation. Other than being about five feet tall, the person seemed normal until he began asking her if she had "seen any shooting stars in the sky".

The witness replied that she often saw shooting stars while out walking her dog and then began to play fetch with the canine. It was then that she saw a "silvery blue object on the other side of the lake". The dog returned with the ball, and the stranger threw it for him, tossing the ball an astonishing five hundred metres (over 540 yards or 1,620 feet).

The witness commented on the man's throwing arm, and as they talked about dogs, fog rolled in, sudden and thick. The woman lost sight of her dog and, concerned for her pet, began to look for him. The animal returned to her, tail wagging, but when the woman turned back to her odd companion, he was gone. Also gone was the strange silvery blue object that she had seen across the lake.

When the witness walked over to where the object had been positioned, all she found was some crushed grass where something heavy had sat.

Once again, we seem to have a case where the fog is either used to obscure the occupants and craft in these incidents or the mist is actually a transport medium. We will turn our attention next to some abduction encounters that will deepen this mystery even further.

ABDUCTIONS

In reading abduction encounters, as strange as they are, we seldom see a narrative where the abduction fails. Abductees are often presented as helpless victims of forces well beyond their control, but there are cases where people have escaped these encounters. My first story will be a historical account of such an escape.

Brad Steiger, in *Strange Disappearances,* gives us the tale of Hans Gustafsson and Stig Rydberg, two Swedes who were driving from Hoganas to Helsingborg on 20 December 1958. Fog had reduced their speed to twenty-five miles per hour, so they were making slow progress.

As the two approached a roadside clearing in the dense forest, they spotted an anomaly and decided to investigate. "An odd shape loomed up out of the mist. It was a disc approximately twenty-five feet broad and a yard high. It was perched on legs about two feet long and strangest of all, it seemed to be composed of light".

The strangeness deepened as the men noted four "things" capering about the clearing. The beings looked like "clumps of mist" but were darker than the [presumably] natural fog. For some reason, in their testimony, the two travellers dubbed these beings "jelly-bags".

The jelly-bags approached the two humans and attached themselves, and a "tremendous force" tried to haul the two into the craft. Rydberg managed to escape the grasp of the jelly-bags and dashed to the car, where he "lay heavily upon the horn in the hope of summoning someone to their aid".

The effect was immediate and beneficial. Gustafsson, who had grabbed a post to avoid being hauled into the craft and was stretched out horizontal in the air, like a pennant in the wind, fell to the ground. The jelly-bags moved to their vehicle and took off with a "high-pitched whistle".

Subsequent police investigation yielded marks allegedly made by the craft in the clearing, and psychologists were convinced that the two were telling the truth as they perceived it, based on some real occurrence.

The sound of a honking horn actually dissuaded these beings from their actions and caused them to flee. I am minded of the UFO in the Knowles case that seemed unable to find the family once the lights to their car were extinguished.

Again, this scenario argues against the extraterrestrial hypothesis (ETH) in my mind. Beings with technology sufficient to bridge the stars ought to be able to catch and subdue a couple of humans without the Keystone Cops approach that these jelly-bags took.

I think that something far stranger than blob-flown spaceships is going on here. An early teacher of mine once described beings that sound exactly like the amorphous jelly-bags. He told me that they were a type of astral parasite, low-level beings of the Otherworld that live on the energy generated by the emotions of humans. This teacher told me that, if one had sufficient psychic ability, one could see these things hanging around "dive" bars, feasting on the anger, despair, and lust so common in such places.

If we turn our minds in this direction for a moment, we begin to see the outline of a different scenario for abductions, one hinted at by writers such as Jacques Vallee and Joshua Cutchin.

Digging deeper into this idea, Joshua Cutchin details a more "traditional" abduction in *Thieves in the Night* that also highlights the difficulty in investigating abduction cases. A seven-year-old girl and her four siblings were staying with an aunt in Litchfield, New Hampshire, in September 1965. All of the children woke to find a "stifling red mist" filling the bedroom where they had been sleeping. This is the sole conscious memory that the witnesses had, and while it is odd, the abduction postscript to the incident was written twenty-five years later.

The primary witness, who had been seven at the time of the incident, was hypnotized in 1990 and told of climbing onto a chair and looking into the eyes of the classic Grey alien. The next memory in the sequence is of the witness and a cousin standing in the yard underneath a "hovering, domed disc". The children were levitated into the craft and, unable to move, subjected to an examination, and then floated back to earth.

I want to make it clear here that I believe abduction experiencers. There is some occurrence happening to these people, they are definitely undergoing something, but, again, I am not sure what the event actually is. It seems to me, though, that a UFO investigator digging at a twenty-five-year-old memory with hypnosis is a recipe for that investigator to hear exactly what they want to hear, especially given the prevalence of Whitely Strieber's *Communion* at that time.

I will note that Strieber states clearly in the book *The Super Natural* that he is not a proponent of the "alien" abduction theory. This book contains a whole extended paragraph of theories about what *might* be behind abduction encounters. While the list includes the aliens-from-outer-space hypothesis, Strieber notes that his late wife Ann, sorting through the many letters they received after *Communion* was published, concluded that the phenomenon had to have something to do with the dead.

So, while I am convinced that abduction experiences are just that, experiences, I think that it is high time that researchers in this area move beyond the idea that aliens are probing humans for some unknown reason, and start to look at the wide boundaries of consciousness research and the input of folklore in these abductions. They might just be surprised at what they find.

Linda Godfrey, Patrick Harpur and Joshua Cutchin all mention the story of the green mist of Aveley in Essex, UK, in their respective works.

A family, John and Susan Day and three children, were driving home from a "social event" one evening in 1974 when they noticed a blue light tracking them amidst the trees. This phenomenon occurred for several minutes and then disappeared only to be replaced by something even more odd – sudden deafening silence and a mass of green fog or mist appearing around their vehicle.

The car radio and its engine stopped for what seemed like a few moments, and then the vehicle restarted, bursting from the fog, although the radio was completely shorted out. The family was shocked to discover that they were farther along the road than they ought to be and that two hours had passed that they could not account for.

The strangeness continued when the parents and their children arrived home. For some reason, the television had stopped working. Family members had nightmares, there was poltergeist-like activity in the home, and unexplainably, the family developed a "strong aversion to meat".

Investigators Andy Collins and Barry King, along with Jenny Randles, looked into the incident and, under hypnosis, were told that the family had been taken into a craft by the tall, blonde, fair, Nordic-type aliens. Interestingly, witness Susan Day, while in the hypnotic trance, seemed to be posing the investigator's questions to the aliens and then supplying their responses. Randles was told that the aliens had genetically engineered humans and visited Earth to monitor their creations' progress.

Witnesses Steven Harris, Stan Gayer and Helen White, along with two others, tell the following tale in Jacques Vallee's *Confrontations.*

The three had experienced an earlier UFO contact event and were looking for answers to what they had seen on 2 November 1975. The group drove up into a canyon at the base of Cade Mountain when they suddenly experienced "an area of heavy fog". Contact with the fog seemed to scramble their recollection, but they did recall boulders falling from cliffs and bouncing around their truck along with the door locks opening and a being telling Harris that he wouldn't need the weapon he was reaching for. The group also believed that they'd spotted a hovering object.

White stated that she was lifted inside a room, but Vallee notes that she was confused about the timing of this encounter. In any event, White remembers, at some point, having a conversation with a being that told her about transparent gold and how it was mentioned in her Bible.

Harris believed that he was in a craft with a clear window that looked out over a mountain he recognized.

I find it interesting that, in two of the three episodes above, the fog or mist definitely preceded the experience. We can't be certain when the red mist appeared to our seven-year-old witness, but given what we have seen so far, the mist might have been a precursor to the experience.

Another abduction story where the percipient puts up a fight is told in *The Vengeful Djinn*. While the late Rosemary Ellen Guiley calls this a possible djinn encounter, I am inclined to place it with our abduction scenarios.

The witness, Martin, was sleeping at about 0200 hours, sometime in the spring of 2007. He awakened from sound slumber to sounds within the house and thought he might have an intruder present. Living alone with no neighbours close by, Martin tried to dial 911, but his phone was dead.

He leapt from bed and waited for the intruders to enter his bedroom. A former military man, he was determined not to go down without a fight. Four small "lizard-looking people" came into his room and stared at him, motionless. When the beings came after him, Martin grabbed one and swung his fist at another. That reptile-looking being vanished into smoke and then re-formed, completely unharmed.

Martin put up a heck of a fight, throwing items at the beings and yelling that he was not going with them, but eventually, one of the creatures subdued him using a yellow light that came from his palm. "Martin was instantly paralyzed and fell back on the bed". The beings approached him, where he lay in the bed, and another yellow light appeared, "followed by some instruments that materialized in mid-air".

Martin's memory blanked at this point, and he woke at about 0900 hours with a "severe headache". Interestingly, he could find no evidence of his night-time encounter despite the fight he had put up, but remained positive that he was not dreaming.

So not only are our "visitors", as Whitely Strieber likes to call them, sometimes preceded by fogs or mists, but it seems that they might not be wholly corporeal. The little reptile in Martin's experience escapes harm by turning into smoke and then re-forming itself, but we are told that Martin succeeded in grabbing one of the other beings. I would simply point out that the djinn are not the only creatures in the endless taxonomy of the Otherworld who are capable of such behaviour.

In his interesting work on the abduction phenomenon, Dr. John Mack examines, in depth, the cases of several abduction experiencers. While Mack is certainly of the opinion that these are alien incursions into these people's lives, the stories of some of the experiencers are rife with fog imagery.

Witness Peter, who was staying with a friend, described an abduction event in Nantucket where a being floated toward his host's bed, causing Peter anxiety that the host, too, would be taken. The host remained in place, but then Peter is told that "it's time to go". A fog came into the room, and Peter stated that the fog chilled him but also calmed him. Peter related that he was always cold during abduction events, presumably because of the aforementioned fog.

I find it fascinating that the fog, in this case, seemed to have a sedative effect, another example of the physiological effects these mysterious mists seem to have.

Mack's subject Ed had an experience where he and his friend Bob Baxter were camping out in the back of Baxter's parents' Nash during a vacation. Ed remembered the fog of the night "shrouding in" and then felt a certain level of psychological discomfort before beginning to fall asleep.

As he started to doze, Ed discerned a tingling sensation at the base of his skull and then felt as though he were floating. A grey fog surrounded him, and the tingling sensation penetrated further into his head before he lost any further memory of the event.

While this incident can only be placed as an abduction due

to Ed's later experiences, a couple of interesting things pop up in this scenario. While the fog in this event may have been completely natural, it is intriguing that the shrouding effect of the fog is accompanied by a "tingling sensation" in one of the energy centres recognized by metaphysical disciplines. I know it as the Alta Major chakra, and Chinese medicine recognizes several important acupuncture points in the base of the skull. This tingling is then accompanied by what sounds like the beginning of an out-of-body experience (OOBE).

In a final Mack case, Sheila was undergoing a hypnotic regression where she saw a light so bright that she asked Mack if he was shining a light on her. The witness reported that she was enveloped in "gray and stuff all around me this is like mist". Unlike Ed, she was not cold and felt as though she was surrounded in a grey, misty, room temperature bubble with "no defined walls or a flat ceiling".

The encounter continued with Sheila feeling that there were multiple beings that she could not see but were restraining her. Then the witness saw "the eyes" and wanted to escape since they were compelling her to look. It seemed evident that some sort of mind control was being utilized.

I was struck, in reading Mack's book, by the idea that each of these cases had fog or mist and that the mist seemed to have different purposes. In Peter's case, it seems as though the fog that enters the room is an agent meant to calm him, while Ed's encounter seems to have a strong OOBE element.

A worthwhile question for investigators of abductions: what relationship does the abduction experience have to OOBEs? For those who practice the form of controlled OOBE called astral projection, the grey fog that Ed experiences can be encountered in what practitioners call the lower astral planes.

Finally, in Sheila's case, the fog seemed to form a container for the experience, almost as if some part of the percipient had been pulled into a pocket dimension, for want of a better name. I was minded of the UFOs that seemed to take their form from the fog in the preceding section of the book.

As a final stop on our quick check of mist-related abductions, Karla Turner, in her volume *Taken*, relates her own chilling encounter, which begins as she is driving home from a visit to her parents:

> … I saw ahead of me on the interstate a large black cloud descending rapidly. It covered both lanes and the shoulders, so there was no way around it, and it appeared so suddenly that I couldn't apply my brakes in time to avoid it. It was daytime, and the darkness of the cloud stood out in stark contrast, with curling edges and a density that made it almost appear to be solid.

Turner had no memory of driving through this suddenly appearing cloud but observed that the smoke-like substance seemed to reach out for her with "finger tendrils". Her final memory of the incident is of being painfully examined though the location of that examination is unclear.

I am struck, in this narrative, by Turner's description of the black cloud as though it were, in some way, sentient. In the next section of this volume, we will examine some stories about mysterious mists, on their own and unattached to another phenomenon, and this seeming sentience will pop up again.

SECTION FOUR

MYSTERIOUS MISTS, TIME SLIPS, TELEPORTATION AND DISAPPEARANCES

MYSTERIOUS MISTS, PART 1

In this section, we will see mists and fogs that have bizarre effects on the people who witness them, but before we plunge into this panoply of weirdness, let's look at a natural phenomenon that sometimes manifests in a markedly strange manner.

According to William Corliss in his book on unusual natural phenomena, scientists say that the polar auroras never descend below fifty kilometres (thirty miles) and are "usually hundreds of kilometres above the surface [of the earth]". Despite the scientific certainty that these light bands originate in and stay in the ionosphere, a number of witnesses testify that this is not so.

Corliss states that "many explorers tell tales of low auroras, even being enveloped in a sea of ethereal white fog". He goes on to cite J. Halvor Johnson who, while exploring Alaska in 1901, observed "an unmistakably low aurora, which was visible between himself and a mountain about half a mile distant, rising to 1,200 feet above his own level". The unusual aurora was accompanied by undefined sounds.

In the winter of 1917–1918, "members of a government radio

station" camping in the Arctic "were enveloped in a light mist or fog-like substance in the aurora; a hand extended could be seen as if in a coloured fog and a kaleidoscope of colours was visible between the hand and the body". Not only were the people in this fog able to see aurora-like lights, but they lay on the ground and find themselves in clear space. The aurora seemingly began four feet above the ground.

Corliss points out that the low auroras are not confined to the high Arctic. Floyd C. Kelley, a student at Trinity College in Hartford, Connecticut, observed a low aurora in the winter of 1908–1909. He said that "the light effects gave me the impression that the atmosphere was filled with fog and someone was illuminating it by playing a searchlight back and forth". The display was so near the ground that the witness felt as though he were walking through "illuminated fog". Kelley also heard a "swishing" sound associated with the display.

Modern-day science still limits the presence of auroras to the ionosphere, high in the atmosphere of the Earth, so I must wonder if the fogs witnessed above were low-lying auroras or, perhaps, the illuminated mists that we will encounter later in this section.

Before we move into specific witness accounts, I'd like to take a moment to mention a mysterious mist from my old stomping grounds in Arizona. Although I could find no witness testimony related to this legendary mist, the tale itself is pervasive, and having visited this area, I can testify that, especially after dark, the place puts up the hackles of many people, even those who do not consider themselves sensitive.

On the *Weird U.S.* website, we find the legend of the Black Mist of Casa Grande Mountain.

Casa Grande is a town located on the way to Tucson from Phoenix, Arizona. The place name, which means Big House in Spanish, is a reference to the ruins associated with the

Hohokam Indians, a tribe that disappeared mysteriously around 1100 CE. Visitors to the region's mountain trail system report a mist that appears "at nighttime on the roads around the base of the mountain. Dark and ethereal, it follows anyone it discovers in the area". The result of this envelopment is said to be "terribly uneasy feelings".

The website goes on to report that their reporter on the ground encountered nothing, but I wanted to include this legend because, as we proceed, we are going to see more of these mists that seem to follow people, try to envelop them, and produce a range of physical and emotional effects. As I've said, I lived in Arizona for a number of years, and I can give first-hand testimony to some of the creepiness to be found in the mountains of that state.

An encounter with a fog that had a profound physical effect occurred in 1956. Author Marie D. Jones, in her book *Modern Science and the Paranormal,* recounts the story of the Coast Guard cutter *Yamacraw.* Retired crew member Frank Flynn reported that the cutter came upon a vapor mass so dense that the ship's powerful searchlight could not pierce it and, indeed, reflected off it. The cutter attempted to "nudge" the mass with its right, or starboard, side, but when the anomaly failed to move, the vessel entered the mass to investigate.

As soon as they were into the fog mass, the ship began to lose steam pressure in the engines. The ship's captain immediately ordered the cutter out of the vaporous mass, and the ship moved away. As soon as the ship exited the vapour, the engines and all electronics returned to normal.

A similar event occurred in 1963 when the American ship *Good News* was hauling an unmanned barge of waste in the Western Atlantic. Jenny Randles, in her book *Time Storms*, a volume that we will be referring to a good deal in the sections to come, reported that Captain Don Henry had the 2,500-ton barge attached to the *Good News* with a line, and the crew were engaged in "routine towing operation[s]".

Henry was called out on deck as the ship's compasses began to spin. A "strange, uniform fog had appeared out of nowhere" on an otherwise clear day and reduced visibility to the point where the crew could not see the barge they were towing. Worse yet, the mist caused the sea and sky to blend together so that the horizon could not be sighted, making even rudimentary navigation difficult.

Henry ordered the crew to move his vessel into clearer air, but the *Good News* was dead in the water, having lost power to the engines and electrical equipment. When the engines finally did fire, the ship was still unable to make way. It was as if "something" was hanging on to the barge and would not let go.

Abruptly, this grasping force seemed to release, and the *Good News* and its tow moved out of the rapidly dissipating fog. Henry sent a party to check the barge, and they reported that all was well "but that the surface of the vessel was unexpectedly hot".

Please note this warmth or even heat to the touch after a fog encounter. We will see this aspect of the mystery again in other incidents. Also prevalent in these episodes is the loss of power – something that we see frequently in UFO encounters as well.

Linda Godfrey in *Monsters Among Us* gives us another 1960s account that veers off in a completely different direction. Citing a book by Preston Dennett, Godfrey relates the story of a woman who lived in the Topanga Canyon area of California and testified that she had seen a "thing made of closely densely packed fog". The witness said that she had seen this thing on two occasions and had gotten a very good look at it. She stated that it "reminded her of a sheep, except where its eyes should have been there were only dark, entirely empty holes that she could look right through to see the landscape beyond".

Godfrey goes on to note that Dennett indicated in his book that he had investigated hundreds of reports of anomalous occurrences in the area, leading one to believe that the Topanga Canyon might be one of the places John Keel would call a window area. What strikes me about this account though is the form that this mystery fog took. Why take on the form of an eyeless sheep? I couldn't help but think of the phantom, dancing cows in an earlier section of the book. Perhaps the paranormal does have a sense of humour.

It almost seems that whatever intelligence was behind this sighting, if any, was trying to appear harmless but didn't quite get the form right. I was reminded of the stories of skin walkers and other shape changers who were said to be able to change their forms but always got some part of the new form incorrect. We see this motif, too, in the folkloric stories of meetings with the Devil, common in Hispanic cultures, where a young lady encounters the Devil as a dashing, handsome young man but realizes her mistake when he is revealed to have chicken feet or hooves.

In *Time Storms*, Jenny Randles demonstrates that our fogs do not simply cause disturbances but can produce real injury.

On 4 April 1966, at approximately 2000 hours, Ron Sullivan was driving for business near Bendigo, Australia. In a field to his right, the man noticed a "fuzzy, phosphorescent mass perhaps fifteen feet across and shining white". As the driver got closer, an even stranger phenomenon began to take form – an oval appeared above the cloud, and a cone seemed to form between the two while "light like a rainbow ran down the side" of the phenomena.

As Sullivan drove toward this odd display, the light from his headlamps began to bend towards the foggy anomaly, and the closer he got, the more his headlight beams bent. Conventional physics says that this is impossible, and, in fact, the only gravitational phenomenon capable of bending light is said to be a black hole.

Nevertheless, Sullivan, trying to compensate for the anomaly with his headlights, moved his car to the left. The driver overcompensated and went off the left side of the road, nearly striking a tree. Fortunately, he realized his mistake in time, swerved to avoid the tree, and got back on the highway without further incident. The two parts of the anomaly moved toward each other and then contracted into a point and disappeared.

In a sad post note to this incident, Sullivan discovered that a young man had been killed in a car accident on that same road two nights later. No other vehicle was involved in the accident, and it appeared that the driver had simply driven off the road and into a tree. Sullivan promptly reported his own near-miss to the police, and it was then that he learned that the other driver had hit the exact same tree that had almost claimed him two nights before.

While it is possible that the second driver's fatal accident had nothing to do with the anomaly that Sullivan witnessed, I think it strains credulity to call this coincidence. Even if the second driver had been impaired or simply fallen asleep at the wheel, what are the chances that person would hit the exact tree that had almost wrecked Ron Sullivan two nights before? I'm not a statistician, but I am betting those would be very long odds.

Gordon Creighton is a writer whom we will return to in the teleportation section of this volume. In one of his articles in *Flying Saucer Review*, he relates what seems to him to be a "near miss" story based on his other writings.

> An elderly British couple ... were interviewed by me last Sunday (September 13, 1970) and they told me they were

> motoring in cloudless weather in Central Wyoming, on a limitless plain, with nothing to see anywhere except flat ground ... Suddenly their car was overhung and partially enveloped by a strange yellowy-creamish-couloured [*sic*] mist that was weaving about them most peculiarly, and was transparent – yet it seemed to have "body" or shape. The lady was driving, and she stepped on the gas and got out of there in a hurry; they were so scared that they didn't even look in their rear-view mirror ...

Creighton notes that, given the conditions and where the couple were driving, this odd mist must have either "materialized around them, or suddenly swooped down on them from directly above". Obviously, this is not behaviour one would expect from a fog or mist, and one certainly wouldn't expect to see such an odd thing on the prairie during a clear day.

Creighton had covered several cases where someone drove or walked into a mist and came out somewhere far away, so we can understand why he viewed this incident as a "near miss". We will save teleportation for later; we still have some more ground to cover with mysterious mists and their varied, unexpected effects.

MYSTERIOUS MISTS, PART 2

Delving further into the realm of unexplained mists, *Time Storms* gives us another interesting incident. Jenny Randles interviewed Patricia Cater, a computer operator who was driving along the A39 near Kilve in Somerset, England, when the techie noticed a strange floating mass north of the road. Curious, Cater exited her vehicle for a closer look, walking across a field and seeing, as she got closer, that the mass she had noticed was, in fact, a cloud-like form in the shape of a large, grey egg.

Continuing to move toward the egg-shaped cloud, she "entered a region where [her] skin prickled and [her] hair stood on end". Randles surmised that the witness had moved into a field of electrostatic charge. Cater went on to say that she felt she was entering an area with a powerful energy to it. "She heard a humming noise emanating from the floating mist and decided not to risk going closer".

As the witness moved away from the cloud form, there was an abrupt cut-off of the energy once she had gotten a certain distance away from the phenomenon. The energy field seemed to end, and the prickling sensation vanished. Cater noted that twelve minutes had elapsed since the time she exited the car, but Randles did not seem to think this was an unreasonable amount of time for the encounter.

Given the unpredictable effects that these mists seem to have on people, I believe the witness made a good choice here. Sometimes, discretion is the better part of valour.

In *Monsters Among Us*, Linda Godfrey spoke to hunter Glenn Arntzen about his experience and the emotional effects these obscurations can have.

Arntzen was out at about 0900 hours during the deer-hunting season of 1985 in the Escanaba River State Forest. The forest is near the community of Helps in the Upper Peninsula of Michigan, and Arntzen had just decided not to take a shot on a yearling deer he had spied. "All of the sudden, the swamp appeared to take on this weird greenish hue," the witness stated. "I mean ... the trees, the ground, the sky all appeared this greenish color. Even the air ..."

The green glow had a definite effect on the deer Arntzen was stalking. It shivered and lay down with its head on the ground. At the same time, the deer hunter was experiencing intense feelings of "sadness, remorse, shame, sorrow" and a lack of will to do anything at all, including stick his head out of the blind and look at the sky.

This strange hue in the air moved over the top of the hunter's blind on its way to disappearing into the swamp. As it did so, Arntzen reported that he "felt it sucking the intense emotion of sad gloom from him and replacing it with a euphoric state". The green glow's passing also seemed to free the deer, which sprang to its feet and ran off toward where the glow was retreating into the swamp.

This odd emotional roller coaster was not typical of the witness, and he reported that he had not had this sort of down, then up emotional response either before or after the event.

During the experience, he also felt that time had slowed down. What was actually only two or three minutes felt like fifteen to Arntzen.

If you will recall, one of the witnesses in the historical section dealing with the faery mentions that a green mist is associated with the fae. In that account, the green mist was seen to waken the earth after the long winter. Deer season is usually in the fall, so is it not possible that a similar mist helps to settle the earth for a winter's sleep? My animistic heart would like to think so.

The rest of the accounts in this section all come from Jenny Randles' excellent book *Time Storms*.

Novelist Martin Caidin, best known for his novel *Cyborg*, which became the basis for TV's *Six Million Dollar Man*, was also a pilot. In 1986, he was piloting a Catalina flying boat across the Atlantic with the plane packed full of skilled flyers – a US Navy pilot, a US Air Force engineer and a captain who flew heavy commercial jets. All told, there were seven witnesses to the incident.

Caidin noted that flight conditions were "perfect", and he was up front while other pilots took a turn at the controls. Not only was this aircraft equipped with a skilled contingent of pilots, on their way back from a European tour, but it also packed the latest in navigation equipment as well as "direct links to a weather satellite that was printing out continual photographic images of the route ahead." Those satellite photos had indicated that the nearest cloud to the plane was over two hundred miles away near Melbourne Beach, Florida.

As Caidin watched, the wing of the aircraft disappeared from view and, abruptly, the plane was flying through "a uniform creamy yellow substance that was clinging to the Catalina". This "eggnog", as the witness called it, seemed to cause "millions of dollars of communications equipment, electronics and radios [to dissolve] into randomly flashing lights and meaningless displays of digits".

With the gyros and compasses spinning wildly, Caidin noted that the fog had a distinct, tube-like shape. The pilot could see sky above and below him. Randles notes that it is a credit to the skill of the pilots on board that they managed to keep the plane in the air with no instrumental way to orient themselves, very limited visibility for orienting themselves in space, or any way to communicate with ground-based air traffic control.

Time, too, seemed to lose meaning, but after about an hour, the Catalina came clear of the fog. The moment that it did, all instruments came back online and appeared to be working perfectly. When the pilots circled to take a look at the strange fog, it had completely disappeared. The plane landed safely in Florida shortly thereafter.

I would be remiss if I didn't note that this incident occurred in the notorious Bermuda Triangle, an area said to be rife with mysterious disappearances of aircraft and ships. Given the strength of this anomaly, this plane should have crashed into the sea, and as Randles notes, it is a testament to the skill of these aviators that they survived the flight.

Both Andrew Nicholson and Jenny Randles tell the story of the Nemingha, Australia, mystery mist.

On 22 March 1976, at 0545 hours, a couple driving home from Murrurundi in New South Wales had stopped in the settlement of Nemingha to check their map and route themselves home. A white car appeared on the quiet road, and the two witnesses got out to try to flag it down, hoping for directions. "A hazy yellow-green light" appeared and enveloped the white car.

It appeared the driver of the white vehicle lost control. The car crossed to the wrong side of the road and was "surrounded by a very localized patch of white haze or mist". The white car coasted along, all power seemingly gone, until it came to a stop.

We are not told why the witnesses did not approach the vehicle at this point. Suffice to say that, after a minute or two, the white haze vanished. A lady dressed in blue got out of the car and tried to clear the windscreen, which was covered in white material, with a yellow cloth. Once she had done this, power returned to the vehicle, without anyone to switch things on inside the car.

The woman driving the white car looked shocked but got into her vehicle and drove off, disappearing in the distance with her car still covered in the white substance that had not been there before the mist. The cloth she had been using to clear her windshield burst into flame on the road where it lay.

This event is intriguing because of its sheer strangeness. I understand that fear might have kept the witnesses from approaching this vehicle, but one is left to wonder what in the world actually happened with the white vehicle and the lady driving it.

What was the source of the hazy light that seemed to cause the car to lose control? Again, what was the source of the localized fog that enveloped the vehicle and appeared to leave a perplexing residue on the automobile? Why did the vehicle come to life abruptly once the windscreen was cleared? Finally, why would the cloth used to clean the glass suddenly burst into flames? The Nemingha encounter is truly one for the unexplained files.

In a completely different sort of incident but one that is no less puzzling, Randles introduces us to Graeme Brock, the headmaster of a primary school in the Peak District of England. On 15 June 1988, Brock spotted what he thought was hay "rising from a field nearby". He went to check this oddity out but found no one there.

Brock was monitoring a game of rounders (a British version of baseball) when he again saw hay floating in the field in defiance of gravity. The children joined him in watching as the hay "spiralled to condense into a solid-looking lens shape". Quickly, the lens shape turned into a "dark grey oval [cloud]" and rose until it seemed that the upward and downward forces were balanced, and the cloud hovered some 150 feet in the air.

The mass began to move across the sky, and additional forces caused it to rotate. Randles notes that, if the mass had been seen at this point, it would have been reported as a UFO.

Brock and several of the children, as the mass hovered overhead and had just begun to move, reported feeling pressure on their shoulders or a tingling sensation. The mass moved over a housing estate and was seen by witnesses there before losing cohesion and coming apart, dumping a significant amount of hay on a golf course while the remainder "drifted away as a strange cloud".

As with so much of the strangeness that we have seen over the course of these explorations, I know of no force that comes along, counters gravity for a time, can form objects floating in the antigravity field into shapes, and then move them along before dissipating. If this sort of thing happens on even a semi-regular basis, it could explain some of the odd things seen in the skies.

In another instance of an antigravity cloud, Randles relates the story of Mark Henshall. The witness was sixteen at the time of the incident on 06 June 1977. Henshall was riding his motorcycle on a rural road in County Durham in the north of England near the town of Lartington. The weather was unusually cold and wet for midsummer, and as Henshall made his way down the road at about 2330 hours, he noted two "purple glows" behind him.

Thinking that the glows were an approaching car, he kept

checking his mirrors for his own safety's sake. A Jaguar motorcar did approach and prepare to pass him, but this was not the source of the purple glows he had seen earlier. He pulled to the right, and the Jaguar was overtaking him to pass when both vehicles were swamped by a "blinding, hazy glow ... a vivid, fuzzy purple colour with a pinkish tinge".

Henshall's motorcycle lost power immediately, and the young man noted that his back and legs were becoming very warm and that his leather jacket was starting to steam. Despite being unable to get a response from the throttle, Henshall and his conveyance were pulled up the hill they were on along with the Jaguar. Randles notes that "both vehicles travelled uphill about 300 feet with the fuzzy glow engulfing them, but with no actual power to do so".

A site reconstruction showed that both Henshall and the Jaguar driver had been pulled over the crest of a small hill. According to the witnesses, the mist simply vanished after this event.

Henshall tried to brake while he was being dragged uphill, to no avail, and, when he touched the metal tank on his bike, it was hot to the touch. Additionally, the young man found that his riding suit was bone dry after the encounter. The driver of the Jaguar confirmed Henshall's story but was so shaken that "he requested anonymity and refused to discuss the matter further than the basics".

What sort of cloud is capable of pulling a motorcycle and even a full-size motorcar up a hill while supplying enough heat to dry out a thoroughly sodden riding suit? Again, I know of no scientific explanation for this event and find it hard to even think of a paranormal explanation for the incident.

In our final story from Jenny Randles, we get to experience snow in May, a rare occurrence even in Canada!

In May 1994 [Norman James] he and his wife were on a

caravanning holiday in Chagford, Devon, in the heart of Dartmoor. At about 3 a.m., Norman got up to go to the toilet and noticed how the clear, moonlit night was disturbed by a strange mist, which formed a "white, vertical, oblong blanket, phosphorescent but giving off no light". Even more peculiar was the fact that it seemed to have deposited what he terms "scatterings" of a white powder, not unlike snow, on the grass immediately beneath. Actual snow is most unlikely, given the weather. The mist was so solid that it hid objects just feet behind it, but was only about fifteen feet long and some five feet high.

When Norman returned to the caravan he told his wife, who came to the door and saw it too. By dawn it had gone. Nor was there any trace of the white powder. Neither the farmer on whose land they were staying nor the local weather centre which they consulted, had ever heard of a phenomenon like this.

Again and again, we keep encountering these shaped mists with unusual properties – strange feelings, emotional lability, interference with electronics, opposition to gravity and more. Now, we will visit visual obscurations that have an even stranger effect.

TIME SLIPS

Andrew Nicholson, in *Weird Australia*, gives us our first account in an even more bizarre and puzzling effect of our paranormal fogs. The witness, J. Truman, wrote a letter to his local paper detailing his experience.

The witness had served in the military "in many parts of the [British] Empire" and relates that he had developed a habit of wearing khakis over those years. Accordingly, he had purchased a pair of khaki trousers from a surplus store and got much more than he bargained for the first time he put them on.

It was a Saturday night, and when the witness put on the pants, "a feeling came over [him] which would be hard to describe". He did not sleep well but rose on Sunday morning, donned the trousers again and proceeded with his day. Presumably, this man was doing some hiking since he relates that he was carrying a haversack and a rifle, but as he made his way across paddocks, he encountered heavy fog, which seemed, for a moment, to intensify.

World War II was only eleven months past, but the witness found himself, without warning, back in wartime, following an Aussie soldier through a jungle setting. The young soldier leading the way was armed, but his tommy gun did him no good as he was cut down by an enemy sniper. The witness recounted that he tried to warn the soldier in front of him, but his yell seems to have set him back into his here and now, scattering sheep and lambs in all directions and making him feel a fool.

The trouser wearer went home and inspected the pants carefully, finding what might have been old bloodstains on them.

If it were not for the inclusion of the intensifying fog, I would label this account an intense episode of psychometry, a psi ability where a person touching an object can relate things about the person or persons who have worn the object. However, since the witness specifically associated the onset of this episode with an intense fog, I am left to wonder. The man says, in the intro to his letter, that he has seen things he could not explain previously, but he does not tell us if he had previous psychic experiences.

Jenny Randles, in the introduction to *Time Storms*, gives us a much more clear-cut case of a time anomaly.

The witness, Dawn, was the wife of a colonel in the Royal Engineers in 1947 Nepal. The colonel and his spouse had decided to take a trip to Tibet to see the Dalai Lama and were travelling with an escort of battle-tested Ghurkha soldiers when they were met with a blast of icy coldness, a common phenomenon in hauntings.

"As soon as the strange sensation struck, I looked up. It was apparent that the others were feeling it, too," the witness stated. "Then I felt as if something was touching me. The Gurkha nearest me reacted. My skin was tingling. It was like a prickling sensation growing stronger ..."

We've encountered this odd physical sensation before, and

we will see it again. It often seems to be a precursor to high strangeness happenings.

The party noticed a "strange red object" approaching, and the local natives, who had come out to greet them, fled. The Brits and their escort later found out that the locals had prior experience with this phenomenon. Even the combat veterans in Dawn's group froze, but after a moment, training kicked in, and her husband grabbed a rifle, ran a few paces, and then seemed to hit an invisible wall. The impact was hard enough to take him out of the fight for the duration of the event.

Dawn, for her part, was unable to look away from this "object", nor could she move. "It did not seem to have any particular shape ... It was a very strange cloud. It was moving just above the surface – but definitely moving. I would say that it was as big as a large house".

The cloud, as though sentient, seemed to home in on Dawn's truck, scattering villagers and Ghurkha guards alike, many of whom sought refuge in the vehicles of the convoy. The cloud circled Dawn's coach "as if performing a military inspection", and a strange pressure in the air accompanied the mysterious cloud. The trucks were actually vibrating, and the prickling sensation noticed earlier became even more profound until it felt almost like an electrical shock.

Another symptom of the "Oz Effect" – a sense of timelessness – also seemed to prevail. Dawn remembers the cloud as moving about and seeming to change shape and colour until it was simply a "grey, floating mass". Dawn perceived that only a few moments had passed, but when things began to return to normal, it was growing dark when it had been broad daylight before.

The colonel, though he had been unconscious through the event, experienced some dizziness and sickness but was otherwise unharmed. Those closest to the cloud, however, experienced nausea and a rash on all their exposed skin, which lasted for a couple of days. After some discussion, once all were recovered from the ordeal, the decision was made to return to their home base and not try to continue on to Tibet.

Given the trying circumstances of travel in those days, one can hardly blame the party, particularly since they had no assurance that the anomaly, whatever it was, wouldn't return with even worse effects. Personally, I might have taken the incident as an omen that visiting the Dalai Lama was not something to do at that particular time, and, in fact, Dawn does state that she did eventually get to meet His Holiness later in life.

In a more modern account from *Time Storms*, Jenny Randles gives the account of a pair of Finnish fishermen who, on 31 July 1981, at approximately 2040 hours, were indulging their hobby on Lake Pielinen. They were headed back to shore near Lieska "when something strange happened".

"A black floating mass appeared above them in the sky", and as it grew closer, the men stated that it looked like a "ball of fog or mist". There were "two glowing lights" inside this mass of mist. One of the fishermen testified that he felt paralyzed though it is not clear whether this was the result of fear or some power exerted from within the fog.

Both men stated that there was a "reality jump", and though they seemed to have shifted places in the boat, they did not remember doing so. The sky seemed lighter than it had before the event, and though they had not changed position relative to the shore, despite strong local currents, they discovered that it was now 0410 hours.

The two fishermen had somehow lost seven hours "in the blink of an eye".

This time loss was quite eerie enough, but the two men also suffered drastic physical symptoms after the event with loss of coordination, shaking hands, inability to walk properly, and lack of balance showing that their neurological systems were affected by the anomaly.

I want to stress again that, according to conventional science, such incidents are impossible. One doesn't simply float into a black cloud and lose seven hours. Even if, as seems to be the case in some abduction cases, the mist or fog had a soporific effect and simply rendered the men unconscious for a long period, then why did their boat not move at all in that time? Even discounting the local currents, a boat will move on a calm lake over the course of seven hours.

Time Storms also gives us the tale of a forty-four-year-old man with the interesting name of Peter Rainbow. His incident occurred in 1983.

After visiting his infirm mother in the village of Little Houghton, UK, Rainbow was riding home on his motorcycle at about 1845 hours, travelling along the A428. As he came round the bend near Great Houghton, his vehicle, lights, and engine died.

Assuming that he had blown a fuse, the witness tried to jury-rig a repair and, when that failed, sought to replace the fuse, again to no effect. It was then that he noted a white, egg-like, glowing mist in a field near him. Rainbow experienced full-on Oz Effect silence, saying, "Everything was quiet. There was no noise at all. No birds. No cars. Nothing. I felt almost in a trance."

The egg-shaped mist moved "like a spinning top" in the field and then "in a blur it was gone". Rainbow abruptly returned to his normal consciousness to find that he was no longer holding the fuse he had been about to replace but was instead holding his keys, which had been in the ignition. When he tried to start the bike, it fired up normally, but when he drove into Little Houghton again, the village clock read 2030 hours. The witness had lost an hour and a half.

I find this account particularly interesting since at no time does the witness indicate that he came into contact with this fog phenomenon. Instead, it almost seems as if the top-like motion of the anomaly put the witness into an altered state of consciousness. This would certainly account for the missing time, but why would no one, including local law enforcement, stop to check on this stranded biker on the side of the road? And how did the witness move from holding a fuse to holding his ignition keys with no memory of changing the two out? If Rainbow was in a trance, then who or what prompted him to make that change?

Linda Godfrey, in *Monsters Among Us,* has a witness who saw a mist anomaly not once, but twice and had time issues in the first encounter. Interestingly, this report comes from a police officer whom Godfrey calls Kevin. The two sightings happened in 2011 and 2012 respectively and took place near the town of Burlington, Wisconsin.

The officer was parked in his patrol car adjacent to a marsh just north of Burlington, working on the inevitable paperwork from a duty shift. He wasn't sure where the mist appeared from. It was just suddenly there, "a large area of rolling green haze", that wafted in over the cattails of the marsh. The green haze moved toward the officer "as if on a mission of its own".

Kevin observed the haze as it drifted in a northwesterly direction, but things began to get strange as the haze approached his car. The electronics on his police vehicle began to malfunction. The engine RPMs dropped to a point just above the place where the engine would have cut off. The headlights dimmed, the onboard computer shut off, and the police radio appeared to be dead as well, despite being fully charged for the shift.

This effect continued as the mist changed course and headed north, vanishing amongst the trees. Once it was gone, all the electronics in the vehicle, including the radio, returned to normal, but Kevin had lost some time:

> "I do not know the time span of this event," said the officer. "I never looked at my watch. However, when I parked in the lot there was still pink in the sky to the west. When the haze was gone, [the sky] was dark, black, and it was near the end of the shift, about ten p.m. Luckily, I was not dispatched to any calls at that time [since] I would not have been aware of them due to the fact none of my communication equipment worked … Looking back on it now, the period that the haze was near me seemed to be a very short time span, but it seemed as though the end of my shift came too quickly. I did not realize that at the time. I base this on the fact that I pulled into the [lot] just after the sun had set [and] it seemed as though the haze left as quickly as it showed up. At the time this seemed as though it was a matter of minutes, but looking back on it, crazy as it may sound, it could have lasted for a half hour. I do not really know."

Kevin had his 2012 run-in with the green haze under similar circumstances only this time he was east of town in Fischer County Park near a boat ramp at Browns Lake. In this event, he did not come in contact with the mist, and his vehicle electronics were not affected. He does state, however, that he is not certain how long the event lasted but feels that it was only a few minutes.

While Kevin's account is not as spectacular as some of the others above and he seems to have only lost a short period of time, I found his story compelling because of who he is. Police officers, like pilots and members of the armed forces, are trained to observe. I was interested to note that Kevin observed this anomaly floating over a swamp near him, and his response was simply to observe the haze, even as his car electronics failed.

Please understand that I am not being critical of the officer. I feel that perhaps that dampening effect noted on the electronics was also affecting the electrical signals in the human brain. We've seen instances where a fog or mist produced emotional responses and others where people just blanked out.

I think this fog induced a passive mental state since I don't know any police officer who encounters something odd and doesn't look at their watch. A time check is essential since you know you may be writing a report on the incident later. It's a habit that anyone in security or law enforcement picks up quickly in training.

We've seen strange fogs and mists that have produced a variety of effects so far, ranging from a prickling, electrical sensation to a loss of consciousness and later nausea to missing time that occurs when the witness comes close to one of these mysteries or actually enters it.

We are going to move on now to episodes that are so incredible that they simply would not be believed if multiple witnesses hadn't reported them – incidents involving the movement of people and even vehicles from one place to another, distant place.

TELEPORTATION

As you might expect, we will kick off this section of the text with a historical story from Jenny Randles' *Time Storms:*

> The annals of Song-Zi Xian county in China relate how on 8 May 1880 a local farmer, Ju Tan, came upon a misty light in some bushes. He described feeling very strange, including a tingling paralysis, and that there was a humming/rushing noise. He then found himself floating upwards and lost all sense of time and space. His very next recall – as if it had been a moment later – was of being found in a dazed state by a forester in Guizhou province. This was 300 miles from his farm, and two weeks had simply gone by "in a blink".

This story is made all the more incredible by the fact that there were no modern conveyances that could whisk Ju Tan three hundred miles to a new location in those days. Even if the man had possessed a horse, not likely for a poor farmer in China, it would take a normal horse at least six days to make that journey. This is a case of "it could be done by normal means, but why?"

Leaving one's fields alone for two weeks could spell the difference between starvation and making it through another year. Why would a man who relied on those fields go wandering off on an adventure that would take up a month or more of his time and bring him to the attention of the authorities, something that Chinese peasants sought to avoid at all costs?

We have encountered the tingling sensation, odd noises, loss of time sense and change of consciousness in previous mist encounters, but now we are faced with a new aspect of these cases – the feeling of floating upward. It almost seems, in this narrative, as if this poor farmer were literally taken up in a cloud and deposited somewhere else.

The next three accounts come to us from author Gordon Creighton, writing on the subject of teleportations in the *Flying Saucer Review*.

An Argentine businessman, travelling for his work, stopped in Bahía Blanca, a name we will hear again, for the night. He was preparing to depart the place the next morning when "a cloudy mass [enveloped] the whole car". It is unclear whether the man lost consciousness or not, but when he came to himself, he found that he was standing "in some deserted spot in the countryside" without his brand-new car!

The businessman hailed a passing truck driver and asked if he could catch a ride to Bahía Blanca. To his astonishment, he found that he was in Salta, an area 1,155 kilometres (718 miles) northwest of Bahía Blanca. Even more stunning, when the witness checked his watch, he found that only a few minutes had elapsed since he got into his car to continue his journey.

The truck driver took the man into town, and the businessman consulted with the local authorities. They telephoned the police of Bahía Blanca, who, after getting the registration information for the vehicle, checked at the hotel and found the car sitting a "few metres from the hotel, with the engine still running ..."

Remember, please, that this was in 1959. Even today, there is no way for a person to travel over seven hundred miles in a matter of minutes. Let's say, for fun, that this businessman had a time-travelling friend who brought with him the latest supersonic fighter jet from the modern day. Even if the witness had gotten straight out of his car and into the cockpit of this faster-than-sound conveyance and we could skip the business of taking off and getting the fighter up to speed, it would still have taken that fighter jet a little less than twenty minutes to clear the seven hundred plus miles to Salta.

In other words, there is literally no conveyance, even in 2021, that could have gotten the businessman to Salta in "a few minutes". Again, it appears that this witness was simply taken up in a cloud and deposited somewhere else.

In two Brazilian stories from 1968, Creighton drives his point home.

In the first, Sr. Marcilo Ferraz and his wife were driving south from Sao Paulo. As they neared the border between Brazil and Uruguay, they encountered a white cloud on the road. There seems to have been some change in the couples' consciousness, for when they "woke up again", they found themselves in Mexico, a distance of several hundred kilometres!

Both people involved suffered severe traumatic shock. Unfortunately, Sr. Ferraz began to be so infirm that further tests were run, and it was discovered that he had a brain tumour. The witness shot himself shortly thereafter.

This is a very sad postscript to the event, but one can't help but wonder, given the sometimes terrible physical effects we see from these clouds, if this teleportation didn't contribute to the poor man's physical malady and/or his profoundly depressed psychological state.

Almost the exact same thing happened to two young men travelling by jeep in the area of Rio Grande do Sul. Somewhere near Pôrto Alegre, they, too, came upon a "bank of white fog" and wound up in Mexico. The year, again, was 1968.

John Keel in *Our Haunted Planet* gives yet another 1968 story out of the Bahía Blanca area:

> In May 1968, Dr Gerardo Vidal and his wife said they were driving outside the city when their auto was caught up in dense fog, and they lost consciousness. They came to on a strange road. Their watches had stopped, and the surface of their car was badly scorched. They soon learned that forty-eight hours had passed, and they were now in Mexico, many thousands of miles north of Bahia Blanca ...

The scorched surface of the car immediately brings to mind the Henshall case, discussed earlier, where a soaked motorcyclist finds himself dry and discovers that the fuel tank of his bike is hot to the touch after an encounter with a cloud that literally dragged his motorbike and a Jaguar automobile up a hill. One might wonder if young Henshall narrowly avoided ending up in some far-flung spot as well.

Keel goes on to demonstrate that it is not always people in cars who end up at distant locations. Creighton mentions this case in his articles as well.

Eleven-year-old Graciela del Lourdes Gimenez of Cordoba, Argentina, encountered a mist cloud while playing outside her home on 4 August 1968:

> "I wanted to go back indoors and watch TV," she told reporters ... "and then just as I was about to turn around ... a white cloud, like mist, appeared on the front path. It gradually came towards where I was, and then I could no longer see the other houses, and I couldn't move or call out to Mummy ... And after that ... I don't know anything more ... until I found myself on a square where there were lots of people and lots of little boys ..."

The child, uncertain where she was, knocked at a nearby home, and the residents called in the police. No one could figure out how the child got the several miles from her home to the centre of Cordoba, but, at least, in this instance the disappearance had a happy ending, and the child was returned unharmed to her family.

Jenny Randles gives us another teleportation tale in *Time Storms*, this one from Ojebyn, Sweden, 20 September 1971.

Sten Ceder was proceeding down the E4 in north Sweden when he noted a peculiar lightening to the sky, almost like the "atmospheric ionization" that precedes aurora displays. In this case, though, a curtain of light shone down on the road before the witness, in the form of "vertical beams", and encircled the man's car.

The lights were accompanied by a force that Ceder could not properly define but which left him profoundly uncomfortable. Similar to our antigravity clouds seen earlier, when the witness tried to hit the brakes, his car failed to respond, as though it were being pulled forward.

Ceder then testified that, "Everything became black around me. The blackness seemed to be a dense, floating mass of smoke that lay around me so that it was impossible to see anything." The smoke also seemed to have an effect like a black hole in outer space, absorbing all light.

The witness swung his vehicle to the left, hoping to get out of the smoke by taking an exit, but, instead, a moment later he emerged from the smoke. He was some distance from where he expected to be. The black cloud was rising from the road into the sky but still seemed to "... erode all ambient light in its vicinity ..."

In *Modern Science and the Paranormal,* Marie D. Jones relates an episode that took place in the so-called Bermuda Triangle, a place of mystery that we already encountered in the remarkable story of Martin Caidin.

Bruce Gernon Jr., his father, and a business associate of the two men were flying a Beechcraft Bonanza A36 aircraft out of Andros Airport in the Bahamas en route to Florida. Gernon stated that, not long after take-off, he noted a lenticular (lens or saucer-shaped) cloud at about five hundred feet above the ocean. The weather reports were good, but as the witnesses watched, the cloud became a large cumulus formation that seemed to be rising at the same rate the aircraft was ascending.

The cloud swallowed the plane, and the pilot, Gernon Jr., could not find any clear air until he reached an altitude of 11,500 feet. Another cloud was building in front of the plane, and upon entering this cloud, despite the good weather reports, the pilot and his passengers could see that the cloud was "dark and black, without rain". The obscuration was full of "extraordinarily bright flashes" that revealed to them that the cloud masses they had encountered were part of the same ring-shaped cloud.

After another thirteen miles or so of travel, the witnesses encountered a "u-shaped opening, which closed into a hole as they approached it". While inside this "tunnel", the pilot experienced feelings of weightlessness, and all of the electronic and magnetic instrumentation ceased to function. Once out of the cloud formation, Gernon was able to contact an air traffic controller in Miami. After some more issues, the controller was able to place the aircraft over Miami Beach.

The trouble was the pilot's watch told him that somehow his aircraft had flown 250 miles in forty-seven minutes.

The top speed for the aircraft is a little over 200 miles per hour, and its normal cruising speed is 193 miles per hour. At the normal cruising speed, not counting time to take off and accelerate, this plane should have travelled no more than 151 miles. Even at its top speed of 206 miles per hour, the plane could have gone no farther than 161 miles. How then did it end up over 250 miles from its take-off point? Given the massive instrument failure in the Caidin story and this story of teleportation combined with instrument failure, is it any wonder that planes and ships go missing in this region?

Returning to Jenny Randles, we also have the story of the Woburn Sands teleportation incident on 8 August 1992. The Smiths – mother, father and two young daughters – had been out shopping and were nearing Hockliffe in the UK when things became distinctly weird.

The family had been amusing themselves by singing Beatles songs, but suddenly all of them seemed to turn within, stopping their singing in mid-song, as "quietness [fell] over the car". In another example of the Oz Effect, the silence seemed to fall over the car and then translate outside the vehicle as all traffic disappeared.

The vehicle was shrouded in a very localized, very damp mist so that the family had extremely poor visibility. At that point, as we see so often, things abruptly returned to normal. The sounds reappeared, and the traffic around them was as it had been before the incident.

The witnesses were very disoriented, however, when they realized that they were in Woburn Sands, some eight miles from the spot where they had encountered the mist. It seemed to all of them that one moment they were in one place, and the next moment, they were somewhere else.

Randles notes that it took a while for the feeling of time having altered to dissipate and that the children were quiet for some hours after the incident. Both parents suffered neurological symptoms, including loss of coordination, tingling sensation with muscle pain bordering on paralysis, shooting pain and red rashes on their hands that took a day to fade.

As we've seen, exposure to these mists can be quite deleterious, even in a relatively brief encounter like this one.

Finally, Lon Strickler's *Phantoms and Monsters* gives us another mysterious fog story that involves a trucker named Chris who was driving in Delaware at the time of his incident.

> I was driving eastbound on Interstate 70 through Ohio and there's an interchange of interstate 77. It goes north and south and I was going east toward that, wide awake. I drive a brand-new truck. I had plenty of sleep. Driving conditions were perfect. I could see stars in the sky and a partial moon. It was very bright. Then, as I got close to [the] interchange, there was some slight fog but it wasn't anything too drastic, it was just minor but, you know, like, to make a long story short, the last thing I remember is approaching this interchange and what seemed to be like, exactly like, maybe 2 or 3 seconds. I'm out of the fog and about 2 or 3 minutes after that, I noticed the mile marker signs being different, meaning, instead of being 81-82-83 they were 37-38, that way ... lower sequence and I noticed that the moon, that was in front of me, was out to my left, so I was obviously going south.

As the witness said, long story short, the driver entered the fog bank and, approximately thirty-seconds later, found himself fifteen miles away from the interchange that he had just been approaching. Fifteen miles in thirty-seconds would be about 1,800 miles per hour, so I don't think the truck was moving that fast. Once more we have an instance where a vehicle drives into a cloud or fog and ends up some distance away. I suppose, given some of the stories above, that Chris is lucky he did not end up in the Midwest or even Mexico.

We have seen cases, over the course of history, where people entered our mysterious mists, fogs or clouds and ended up in an entirely different location. Sometimes, those locations were only a few miles from where the witness entered the obscuration, but we have also seen examples of people being transported hundreds of miles with no evident mechanism of travel.

These experiences are frightening enough, but we also need to examine some stories that could have direct relevance to mysterious disappearances throughout the world.

DISAPPEARANCES, PART I

Investigating disappearances is truly frustrating since, when someone disappears under mysterious circumstances and does not reappear, we obviously do not have witnesses to the actual event. We may have witnesses who saw the disappeared shortly before they vanished, or people who were actually in a party with the disappeared who then lost track of the person who was lost. In almost all cases of mysterious disappearance, no one sees the person disappear. The best we can hope for is a scenario where there is physical evidence of the vanishing such as the classic footprints leading to nowhere.

In the episodes where an individual disappears mysteriously and then is found, we have another set of circumstances that contribute to confusion around those disappearances. While cases of people who have gotten lost and then been found are commonplace, the lost person in these cases knows they were lost and can account for the time that they were gone. In what have become known as Missing 411 cases, after the David Paulides books, however, the lost person who is recovered has little or no memory of the time they were gone or gives an account that makes investigators shake their heads in puzzlement.

A terrific example is the case of three-year-old Casey Hathaway, a child who disappeared in the forests of North Carolina. Hathaway had been playing with two other relatives in his great-grandmother's backyard and failed to come in when the others did. The boy's disappearance sparked a search and rescue effort that included teams from across the state, federal resources, helicopters, drones, and canines.

Searchers were very concerned since the overnight weather conditions during the search were below freezing, and the child was not dressed for extreme cold. On day three of the search, the child was located, nestled in "a mess of vines and thorns". Medical personnel stated that the child offered only one factoid about his time away from home: Casey Hathaway told the hospital staff that he had been cared for by his friend who was a bear.

We may never know what actually happened to Casey Hathaway, but one thing seems clear, most three-year-olds would not have survived the freezing conditions without some sort of shelter. Now, it may be that the young one found a place to hole up and stay warm at night, but this is not an action one would expect from most three-year-olds. It seems likely that Hathaway's "friend", which he perceived as a bear, helped shelter him. Sasquatch? Or something even stranger?

While the Hathaway case does not have a fog or mist component, the lore of mysterious fogs and mists provides us with some interesting accounts of people who disappeared completely, in front of witnesses, or who disappeared and then were recovered.

Joshua Cutchin gives us this brief but very sad story in *Thieves in the Night:*

> According to Ukrainian researcher Andrew Zabava, a family cabin in Russia was approached in 1914 by an unnatural fog that alit in a nearby field. The owners were shocked when they realized this was the exact location their son and daughter were playing moments before. The children were never seen again – their parents believed they had been taken by "wood goblins."

Now, we don't know for certain what these folks meant by a "wood goblin", but given our extensive discussion of faery lore earlier, it seems clear that these people believed that some species of fae had carried off their children. The faery folk have a long, sad history of being blamed for such events and even of leaving "changelings" behind to replace children. There is extensive faery lore on how to recover a lost child should one discover such a changeling, but, unfortunately, the lore reveals that it is extremely difficult to recover a person, child or otherwise, once the faery have taken that person away.

In *Strange Disappearances,* Brad Steiger relates two extremely odd tales of disappearances involving a strange mist or cloud.

The first story is from 1933 when Father Litvinov opened the door of his church to an unexpected midnight visitor. The stranger was near hysteria, but, once the priest calmed the man, a strange tale emerged.

The visitor gave his name as Dmitri Girshkov, and according to the young man, who was ornately dressed, he was to be married that day.

On his way to the church, Girshkov had stopped by the local cemetery to pay his respects to an old friend and was startled by an apparition of the friend, who had been dead for some time. As so often happens in these strange cases, the next thing

Girshkov knew, it was evening, and as he made his way back to the Siberian village, he was terrified to discover that almost everything had changed.

At this point, Girshkov again became overwrought and fled the church, yelling that he had to find his friends, family, and bride. The priest "became aware of a strange light and gray mist. In the blinking of an eye, the curiously dressed young man had vanished".

Father Litvinov was shaken enough by the experience to do some research and found records of two other priests of the parish who had seen the exact same thing. He also found the story of Dmitri Girshkov, a young man who disappeared in 1746 on his way to his wedding.

If we had a record of young Girshkov dying at his old friend's grave, then we might suspect that this was a very powerful residual haunting, but there is no such indication. From the young man's words, he simply had a period of missing time and then returned to his village to find everything changed.

This story bears a strong resemblance to tales in faery lore where an individual is carried off by the fae or enters their realm voluntarily. The person eventually begins to pine for their family and is released from faery, usually with some stipulation, such as not dismounting from a horse. The human returns to their home village and discovers that many years have elapsed despite their feeling that they have only been away for a few days or weeks.

The faery are profoundly related to the dead, in the Celtic tales, so one might even view his friend's grave as an entry into that mysterious Otherworld where time passes very differently from time on our plane. Why the young man periodically made appearances at the church is anybody's guess.

The second story from *Strange Disappearances* has more of a UFO flavour to it.

As we've mentioned previously in this volume, Brazil is host to a number of hostile UFO encounters, and this episode is a standout. On 20 August 1962, in Duas Pontes in the state of Minas Gerais, Brazil, young Raimundo de Aleluia Mafra was outside, retrieving his father's horses. The boy had been disturbed in the night by a strange silhouette floating through the house, reminiscent of what we call shadow people now, and was still nervous after the encounter.

His nervousness was not abated by the sight of two "balls" floating three feet above the ground. He described them as large, with one being black and the other black and white. The balls had odd "antenna-like protuberance[s] and a small tail". Both objects hummed and possessed a light source within that resembled the flickering of a firefly or someone turning a light switch on and off rapidly.

The boy, of course, cried out for his father, Rivalino, who came out to see what the matter was. The two objects reportedly merged, gained some altitude, and then discharged a yellow smoke. The now larger ball moved toward the father as his son watched in horror and, when it was upon him, discharged more of the yellow smoke. According to Steiger, an acrid stench filled the air, and when the smoke dissipated, Rivalino Mafra da Silva had completely disappeared.

We have seen these mists associated with missing time and the abduction phenomenon, but it is rare to see a case where the unidentified object so brazenly removes someone from the face of the earth. If the year for this sighting were not 1963, one might suspect that the objects were drones of some type, but that still would not explain the disappearance.

As I noted above, hostile UFO encounters seem to be more

common in Brazil than elsewhere, but we have no explanation of why that is. Was the smoke the medium for removing Rivalino Mafra da Silva from his field, or was it simply an obscuration so that whatever removed the father could not be seen?

We've already mentioned Gordon Creighton, who provided *Flying Saucer Review* with articles on the teleportation phenomenon. Creighton also gives this interesting story, which was cited by John Keel in *Our Haunted Planet:*

> Shortly after 8 a.m. on 19 November 1963, a Mr. Kinoshita [Fuji Bank, Tokyo, Japan] was driving along the Fujishiro by-pass. He was ... headed for a golf-course at Ryugazaki, Ibaraki-ken [north of Tokyo]. In the car with him were two passengers ...
>
> Ever since passing through a place called Kanamachi, they had had in view another car, which was travelling in the same direction. It was a black car ... and it had a Tokyo registration number (which, of course, most unfortunately none of them memorized). In the left-hand rear seato [*sic*] [of] this black car was an elderly man, who was reading a newspaper.
>
> Suddenly, a "puff of something gaseous, like white smoke or vapour, gushed out from somewhere around the black car" and when this cloud dispersed (a matter of not more than five seconds) the black car had vanished.

Of course, newspaper coverage of this incident suggested that the whole thing was a hallucination, but I find that hard to believe since all three witnesses would have had to hallucinate the same thing. Why would three men, out for a relaxing day on the links, suddenly start hallucinating, hallucinate one specific occurrence between the three of them, and then apparently return to normal consciousness, none the worse for wear?

Jacques Vallée relates a very interesting account of a mist-related disappearance that involved the police and had multiple witnesses. He tells the tale in *Revelations,* and it is set in Pontoise, France, on 25 November 1975.

Three friends – Franck Fontaine, Salomon N'Diaye El Mama and Jean-Pierre Prevost – were loading a Ford Taurus with items to take to the market and sell in Gisors. It was 0400 hours when they spotted a "strange, luminous object in the sky". Fontaine decided to see if he could get a closer look while El Mama and Prevost returned to the apartment for a last load and a camera.

Prevost was irritated when he looked out the window to see if he could spot the object from his apartment. What he saw, instead, was that the Taurus, which had no starter and needed to be push started, was sitting on the side of the road with the engine off. Grumbling at the thought of having to push start the car again, Prevost came down to find El Mama very excited, as he had seen "a large sphere of fog engulfing the car". This fog sphere was confirmed by an independent witness known only as Lisette in a later report as well as by the first officers on the scene.

Prevost and El Mama found the car, as described, "surrounded by a large ball of whitish fog around which three or four smaller shares [*sic*] were moving. These spheres entered the large ball, which itself was absorbed into a cylinder that flew off in the sky at a very high speed".

The two young men were unable to locate Fontaine and called the police, who, at first, treated the matter as a hoax and then began to suspect that the two had murdered their friend and dumped his body somewhere. Fortunately for them,

Fontaine reappeared five days later, extremely disoriented and with several days' growth of beard on his face.

The missing man remembered being approached by a luminous object, "about the size of a tennis ball", which stopped over the hood of the vehicle. The engine died, and Fontaine remembers being engulfed in fog so thick that he could see nothing before his eyes began to itch and then grow heavy as he drifted off to sleep. He had no memory after that until he woke in the cabbage field where he was found.

Again, we have a mysterious mist or fog with a very clearly defined area – it was repeatedly described as a sphere – that appears as someone disappears. The item I find really interesting in this account is the sudden contraction of the sphere into a cylinder, which then flies off at high speed. It is entirely possible that this is one of the rare instances where an abduction event had witnesses and seems to show that, at least on occasion, the visitors do physically remove people from the scene of the event.

As we move into more modern times, we have further stories of people disappearing into the mist.

DISAPPEARANCES, PART 2

Not all cases of disappearance involve humans. Jenny Randles tells of an incident involving a pet in *Time Storms*.

On 9 February 1988, "a former army man", John, who had risen early and gone out to look for farm labour work, was walking home, his quest unsuccessful for that day. He was on a road two miles or so from the town of Oswestry, UK, when he happened to see a woman running her spaniel "just off the quiet road".

The canine was off its leash and cavorting in the verge when its mood changed abruptly. It charged across the road "barking furiously at something", and the witness followed the creature only to find himself encountering a "yellow fog" that glowed and seemed to be about forty-five feet in diameter.

"It [the mist] straddled the hedgerow and the path at the side of the road". The fog seemed to be rotating, producing a sort of mini-whirlwind and a sound like rushing wind. The spaniel charged headlong into the mist and vanished though the witness was unclear about whether the dog disappeared or was obscured by the fog.

The woman promptly became hysterical over the loss of her

pet, and John tried to calm her. They both noticed a terrible "sulphurous" stench, the "eerie stillness" that we have encountered so often before and, as we also might expect, an "electric tingling" in the air that made their hair stand on end.

Randles notes that no one monitored the time of this incident, but in what seemed like a short period of time, the fog disappeared, and the two people found the dog unconscious "with its body on the path and it[s] head on the kerb". The witness noticed that the dog was very warm and soaking wet. Steam was rising from the animal is if it had just gotten out of the bath, and it was panting heavily, its eyes red and bloodshot.

John helped the woman place her dog in a vehicle, cover it with a blanket, and the dog owner drove off without a further word. John "noted the details of the car" so that he was able to contact the woman and verify that the spaniel did recover within an hour. When last he had seen the dog, the witness had been certain that the animal was not long for the earth.

All I can say about this story, as a dog lover, is that I am happy that the dog came out of this episode relatively unharmed. We hear so many stories, particularly in cryptozoological circles, of pets being killed during incursions that I was gratified to see this story had a happy ending.

Other than the fact that John faced off with a whirling dervish of a cloud that had all the usual Oz Effect aspects we have come to expect, I was interested to note that the dog was wet and steaming when it was recovered. We have seen, in an antigravity cloud case and a teleportation case, instances where the incident seemed to produce heat in affected objects.

For some reason this effect reminds me of a microwave oven, which causes the water molecules in food to vibrate and thus warms the contents of the oven. We have no idea what sort of mysterious energies may be at work here, but they obviously do more than make things disappear or teleport them to another location.

If you thought you were safe from foggy disappearance at work, you may be mistaken. In a 1996 Florida case, Jenny Randles reveals an incident with videotaped evidence. The incident occurred at a small factory in Florida and was investigated by MUFON personnel, including a psychiatrist, a criminologist, a specialist in physical science and a computer expert.

At 2316 hours, a security guard was monitoring camera feeds from various vulnerable spots on the campus and noted an employee approaching the rear gate. A “fuzzy white glow” arrived and covered the worker, causing what appeared to be electromagnetic interference with the picture. When the “glow” disappeared after two-seconds and the camera returned to normal operation, the employee was gone.

Randles notes that all analysis pointed to the reality of the film images and that a frame-by-frame analysis of the tape showed the “near-instant disappearance” of the worker. The guard went to look for the employee and was unable to locate him. Then, at 0106 hours, the cameras revealed the man’s return.

The reappearance is as sudden as the vanishing. The factory apparently lost lights, and when the “fuzzy glow” appears again, the worker appears within it “a fraction of a second” later. The man is on all fours and quickly becomes “violently sick”.

The guard went out to assist the man, who was disoriented and unable to recall what had happened to him in the preceding two hours. The employee went home, called off sick the next day, and never returned to the factory.

In his shoes, I can’t say that I blame this hapless person. I find it quite interesting that Randles does not recount what happened at the factory in the two hours that the man was gone. A curious silence ensues for this interstitial period.

A man seemingly vanishes, and it is caught on videotape, and then the man reappears two hours later. There is no record of a wider search, the involvement of upper management or law enforcement or even phone calls made to the man's relatives to see if he had slipped out and gone home.

This silence makes me wonder if the guard, fearing for his job or perhaps for his sanity, just tried to ignore the incident and hoped that it would go away (pun not intended). Or, given that the videotape and a covering report were sent to a TV station anonymously, perhaps the security officer was told to keep quiet, but someone at the factory leaked the information.

In another account, Joshua Cutchin's, *Thieves in the Night* cites the *Flying Saucer Review.* The episode is briefly documented but contains some aspects of these cases we have seen before.

> The aunt and grandmother of Rubén Walter Rusin, aged 11, were readying to go downstairs when the boy was enveloped in a dark cloud in the corridor. He was missing for two and a half hours before they found him in the corridor once more. "His flesh was unnaturally warm, and on each cheek of his face ... there was a strange pale red circle," according to an article published in 1997 in *Flying Saucer Review*. Rubén recalled being paralyzed and placed onto "something soft and warm, like a mattress, where something invisible touched him and yelled, 'Talk! Talk!'"

This event could have been placed in either the abduction or this disappearance section, but since the hallmark examination of the abduction experience does not appear, I decided to place the incident with disappearances. Though the boy does seem to have been taken somewhere outside his home, the whole business of something touching him and telling him to talk sounds more like an interrogation than a biological examination. One wonders what was trying to make Rubén talk and what he was expected to talk about.

By now, readers are probably thinking that, if they see any kind of an unnatural cloud, fog, or mist, they had best avoid it, and I would say that is not bad advice. We have accumulated a mass of evidence that shows that these visual obscurations are not to be trifled with and that they can have very real physical effects on the experiencer. In this case, we again see the heating effect that we have noted before as well as marks on the boy's skin.

I was also intrigued by the "soft and warm, like a mattress" place that Rubén described. Unlike an abduction event, which is often described as physically uncomfortable, this boy's abductors seem to have taken care to make him comfortable. Perhaps this was a psychological aid to get the boy to impart whatever information the visitors were looking for?

Author Brent Swancer, in an internet article, gives us some information on Africa's Mount Nyangani, an 8504-foot peak that is called, by the locals, the Mountain That Swallows People. The mountain is the highest point in Zimbabwe, and the natives of the region believe that it is inhabited by powerful ancestral spirits. As an animist myself, when the locals tell me that a place is inhabited by any sort of spirit, but particularly ancestral spirits, my first question is, Are people who are not of your culture allowed in the area? My second question, if I am told that I may enter, is, What offering or actions must I take to ensure that I do not incur the wrath of your ancestors?

As we'll see, that sort of attitude is likely the right one to take especially given that the weather in this area is often said to have a malevolent mind of its own. In addition, Swancer tells us that there are "numerous reports of visitors becoming dazed, confused or disoriented for no apparent reason, with even experienced hikers familiar with the area at times becoming hopelessly lost, as well as sudden bouts of profound dizziness or nausea".

The writer goes on to give a quick tale from earlier in the 1900s where an official party from the government went missing on the mountain and were only recovered after the locals made a sacrifice to the spirits. The officials were missing for four days but thought they had only been gone a few hours.

In November of 2014, however, we encounter the story of Thomas Gaisford who, as the recipient of a college award that funded students "to make rugged treks into remote areas for study", found himself on the slopes of Mount Nyangani. Gaisford was alone on his trek.

At about 1500 hours, the young man was completely enveloped by an "unusually thick bank of fog". Unable to navigate, he wisely chose to pitch his tent and "wait out the strange weather". Gaisford ended up staying overnight and was witness to one of the high strangeness occurrences reported on the mountain. He was watched and circled by various animals who "seemed to almost be keeping an eye on him or studying him".

Thankfully, the student listened to the advice of local villagers and ignored the strangely acting animals. The villagers were clear that such creatures were "not of this world", so Gaisford stated that he:

> ... prayed and slept there for 10 hours. Several scary snakes approached me. I never disturbed them. They came in numbers, but I stood still. Various animals frequented the place and I could see shining red eyes of several animals staring at me. My character was tested. I

> remained steadfast. I woke up the following morning after the fog had cleared. I climbed down before I proceeded to Leopard Rock on foot ...

As a postscript to this encounter, Gaisford noted that he should have consulted the traditional leaders of the villagers before entering the area.

Now, this student did not disappear as did the other people in this section, but I include this episode to illustrate what might be happening when some people enter a fog or mist. What Gaisford describes aligns with journeys into the Otherworld that we see in shamanism, some varieties of traditional witchcraft and even voluntary OOBEs (astral projection). It is clear to all but the most hardened scientific materialist that this young man encountered spirits of some kind and that only his steadfast courage and, perhaps, his faith allowed him to come out of the ordeal unscathed.

Thomas Gaisford was fortunate that he did not become one of the disappeared, and I am heartened to hear that, in the future, he will be more likely to consult the indigenous people of an area before entering their lands.

As always happens when one researches a book like this one, there are stories that should be included but do not slot into the chapter headings that have developed. I am going to cover a number of those miscellaneous stories in the next part of the book.

SECTION FIVE

MISCELLANEOUS STORIES

MISCELLANEOUS, PART 1

Cattle Mutilation

Cattle mutilation cases, by their very nature, are difficult to investigate since there are very few witnesses, and even those witnesses do not see the actual dissection of the animal. One of the leading experts on this phenomenon, Christopher O'Brien, does have one fog-related story in his book *Stalking the Herd.*

O'Brien, in addition to tracking cattle mutilations, has an ongoing project for documenting UFOs in the area of the San Luis Valley (SLV) of Colorado and New Mexico. On 29 November 1997 at 2315 hours, four people witnessed a "a large multi-coloured ball of light bobbing slowly over the northern part of the SLV". The previous day, heavy snow had blanketed the area. On 30 November, dense fog descended into the centre of the valley.

At 0536 hours, dogs alerted at a ranch outside the town of Hooper, which is in the centre of the valley and was, therefore, fogged in.

The following afternoon, a still-warm "mutilated" calf was discovered about five hundred yards from the house, lying in a pristine, untouched snow-covered field. The calf's right-side mandible had been exposed in an arc that went up over the eye socket. The rear end had been cored out in a ten-inch diameter circle, and the coring extended 18 inches into the animal's rear end. Magpies and crows showed an interest, but no coyote or other scavenger tracks were noted around the carcass. The Saguache County sheriff was called, and I visited the site to help investigate this latest peculiar animal death. I obtained video and still footage, three sets of tissue samples and sent the samples off to three different veterinarian pathology labs for testing. Curiously, all three labs disagreed on what the cutting agent was.

On a personal note, I grew up in Texas, had uncles and cousins who were ranchers, and knew any number of people who bred and raised cattle when my dad and I moved out into the Hill Country. Many people do not grasp what an impact the loss of even one animal can be to a small rancher. It can literally mean the difference between turning a small profit that year or having to go into debt trying to keep the place running.

Remember, many of these steads have come down in families for generations, and the family will not willingly give them up. If whatever is causing these awful events decides to home in on a particular ranch, as it did in the San Luis Valley, bankruptcy and loss of the property can result. It's no wonder that there are stories of ranchers taking shots at helicopters and other unknown aircraft after one of these events.

Looking at the mystery itself, there is absolutely no agreement on what causes these terrible dissections. There are many pet theories, ranging from UFO involvement to secret government black ops projects, but no solution is evident even though the fact remains that the mutilators have cost the cattle industry millions of dollars over the years.

The question remains, how does anyone or anything take

livestock, perform surgical incisions on the animal, remove part of its organs and skin, and then replace the dead animal without leaving tracks? Why is it that the carcass left behind seems to be avoided by most scavengers? Of all the mysteries in the paranormal, cattle mutilations are surely one of the scariest and most enigmatic.

Linda Godfrey, in *Monsters Among Us*, has an interesting trail cam story that appears in the introduction to this volume, but she also includes another incident, from 2015, where she was sent photographic documentation of a mutilation near Bloom City, Wisconsin, by retired newspaper writer Steve Stanek. The photos showed "removal of the right leg quarter of one of [the farmer's] cows. It was also surgically precise and round. However, the cow also had suffered classic cattle mutilation marks – a large oval cut away from its jaw and another oval that removed an eye".

Godfrey notes that the photographer, Stanek, had been researching cougars in Wisconsin for years, but that Wisconsin had "no known cougar population", and the surgical precision of the wounds on the animal seemed to belie an attack by a predator. Godfrey also notes:

> Interestingly, two of the three photos from the Bloom City farmer also showed a gray mist hovering over the animal. The third photo, taken in the same series from a different angle, was perfectly bright and clear. Identical mutilations and photos of mists seem curious, indeed!

As you might recall from the introduction, similar mists were seen in trail cams in the Smith case before the disappearance or movement of a deposited animal carcass. While I doubt that a fog or mist is descending on cows and leaving them mutilated, these visual obscurations have certainly been shown to be evident in all sorts of paranormal occurrences.

Crop Circles

Some theorists blame cattle mutilations on UFOs and their occupants, but Christopher O'Brien notes that there could be a lot of other forces behind these terrible acts. The same can be said of another UFO-related topic: crop circles.

As with cattle mutilations, the formation of crop circles happens most often at night and out of the sight of witnesses. This fact alone accounts for the many hoaxes that have muddied the waters of the crop circle debate.

While there are proponents of the idea that these interesting and artistic designs formed by flattened grain are caused by UFOs, a rare witness account, given to us by Jerome Clark in his *Encyclopedia of Strange and Unexplained Physical Phenomenon,* seems to indicate something far stranger going on.

Clark notes that, "daytime witnesses of the formation of simple circles are relatively rare and stand at about three dozen [in 1993, when the book was written]". Clark gives the example of Gary and Vivienne Tomlinson, a couple who were walking near a field of "corn" [an English usage that refers to any cereal grain crop] "near the village of Hambledon". Quoting from the *Mail* on 25 August 1991, the following story unfolded:

> "There was a mist hovering above, and we heard a high-pitched sound," said Mrs. Tomlinson. "Then we felt a wind pushing us from the side and above. It was forcing down our heads so that we could hardly stay upright; yet my husband's hair was standing on end. It was incredible. Then the whirling air seemed to branch into two and zig-zagged off into the

> distance. We could still see it like a light mist or fog, shimmering as it moved."

Clark goes on to tell the tale of a Japanese team of scientists, working with the local Circles Effect Research Group, who were observing a field with a full complement of electronic gear in the summer of 1991. A mist moved in, obscuring visual documentation, and when the mist departed, there was a small "dumbbell" formation in the field. Radar, magnetometers, night-vision video, and motion sensors failed to register any intruders, including humans, in the monitored field.

What force or form is it that moves in these mists and causes these very physical effects?

Men in Black

In his book *Real Men in Black*, Nick Redfern tells the chilling story of Dr. Herbert Hopkin's encounter with a Man in Black (MIB). Dr. Hopkins was a medical doctor who had been involved in the hypnotic regression of an abduction experiencer. On 11 September 1976, the doctor received a call from a man claiming to be with the New Jersey UFO Research Organization, a group the doctor later discovered did not exist.

The doctor, assuming that the call had to do with his latest investigation, politely invited the man over, only to discover the fellow on his porch moments later.

The caller was dressed entirely in black except for grey suede gloves and wore a hat of the same colour. He was extremely pale, and his suit hung loosely on a too-thin body. To make the man even more odd, the doctor noted, when he removed his hat, that the MIB had no hair on his head at all, not even stubble, and was wearing lipstick.

In search and rescue we had a saying, "always trust the dog", and Dr. Hopkins should have done just that. His family collie displayed an extreme fear reaction and wanted nothing to do with this night-time caller.

The MIB spoke with no accent or emotional tone to his voice as he told the doctor that Hopkins had two coins in his pocket and ordered him to take one out. The dark visitor then instructed the doctor to look only at the coin, and the amazed physician watched in awe as the "silver coin took on a blue colour, became blurry, changed from metallic form to a vaporous substance, and finally faded into nothingness".

The truly chilling part of this story is that the stranger then made a veiled reference to the fact that famed UFO abductee Barney Hill "had died because he had no heart, just as Hopkins no longer had the coin". This threat was followed by a demand that Hopkins destroy all records related to the abduction case he was working on.

After this incredible display and the subsequent threat, the MIB got to his feet and tottered to the door, claiming that his energy was now low. After stumbling into the front yard, the MIB was picked up by an unidentified vehicle.

After this event, Dr. Hopkins walked away from the abduction investigation he was involved in, and one can't blame him for doing so. What I wonder in reading about this event is the correlation between turning a coin from its metal form into a smoke-like gas and the sudden desire of this being to be off, since its energy was low. This MIB must have expended a good bit of energy causing that transformation (or holding the doctor in some sort of trance that made him believe the MIB had done this), and one wonders what would have happened if the good doctor had found the courage to challenge this hairless "person" once its energy was depleted.

Mothman

The story of the Point Pleasant Mothman is a long and involved one that has been well covered in other books, most notably the John Keel classic *The Mothman Prophecy*. Cryptozoologist Loren Coleman, in his *Mothman: Evil Incarnate*, includes an odd note that relates to our subject.

On 15 November 1966, two couples from Point Pleasant – Roger and Linda Scarberry and Steve and Mary Malette – had one of the first sightings of the creature that became known as the Mothman near the old munitions plant, called the TNT area, outside town. They described the being as a "large flying man with ten-foot wings" whose eyes "glowed red" in the car's headlights.

Coleman, referring to Linda Scarberry's notes from that time, states that when the frightened group returned to the area with a deputy sheriff, she again saw the creature "out in a pasture". The three accounts that Coleman had access to also mentioned "a cloud of dust or smoke rising from the coal yard near the [TNT] plant".

Could it be that the Point Pleasant Mothman, one of history's most well-known anomalies, cloaked itself in mist as have so many other paranormal entities in this book?

A Sea Monster

Brad Steiger, in *Real Monsters*, quotes a *Fate* magazine article of a fatal encounter with a sea serpent.

On 24 March 1962, Edward Brian McCleary and four friends decided to go skin-diving in Pensacola Bay, Florida. The youths wanted to explore the wreck of the *Massachusetts*, an old naval vessel that had been scuttled in the bay in 1921. The day had been pleasant, but a sudden storm caused the young men considerable trouble, causing them, at one point, to jump over the side of their boat and try to push the seven-foot rubber raft to make some headway. Failing that, they decided to tie off to a buoy.

"A heavy, oppressive fog" settled in the storm's passing, and the sky was darkening. The first sign of trouble was a strong smell of "dead fish", followed by a "tremendous splash" that caused waves to break over the five. The teens were fairly certain the disturbance was not caused by a boat and became certain of it when what appeared to be a ten-foot pole with a head on top broke the water about forty feet from them.

The air was filled with a "strange, high pitched whine", and the nerve of the youths broke. They set out for the section of the *Massachusetts* wreck that was still above water. According to McCleary, all of his friends were dragged under by the creature, and he witnessed the taking of his last friend, a boy named Eric, who was only feet away from him when the monster reared up and then descended on the hapless lad.

McCleary ended up swimming for shore in a blind panic and came to himself later in hospital. The local papers covered the story as a quadruple drowning with no mention of the monster, and the witness states that he was pressured not to tell his story by local officials.

Many of the legendary tales of sea monsters have them destroying ships and eating sailors, but most of the modern sighting accounts I have seen have been just that, sightings. The crew of a vessel report seeing a strange swimming creature in the ocean, record their observations in the ship's log, and go about their day. The serpent is just another oddity of the sea.

I honestly don't know what to make of this story. The witness dropped off the radar after the initial publicity, and it seems that the four boys did indeed disappear, so I am disinclined to think this a hoax.

The ocean is unexplored country, and if I were looking for physically solid cryptid creatures, one of the places I would look would be the approximately 71% of the world's surface that is covered by water.

We don't know what attacked young McCleary and his companions. Relict dinosaur of the plesiosaur family? A giant unknown serpent or eel? The long-necked seal theorized by some sea monster researchers? Until something definitive washes up on shore, we can't say with certainty, but a story of this type makes one consider the wisdom of approaching the ocean in any sort of small vessel.

In the next section of miscellaneous reports, we will encounter everything from a mystery prowler with a gas problem to a tiny mammoth to a possible witness of spontaneous human combustion.

MISCELLANEOUS, PART 2

Mad Gasser of Mattoon

It seems, in a book about paranormal fogs and mists, that I would be remiss in not mentioning this series of incidents in Mattoon, Illinois, in the summer of 1944. Loren Coleman covers this story in his book *Mysterious America.* Again, Coleman and others have done a great job detailing the panic that ensued in Mattoon as these attacks unfolded, but suffice to say that we will see some similarities between the attacks of the Mad Gasser and other mysterious mists we have encountered.

The episodes started on 31 August with a suspicious event involving the partial paralysis of the wife of a sleeping couple. The next day, Mrs. Bert Kearney was awakened by a strange odour at about 2300 hours and, discovering that she was developing paralysis in her lower body, called for help. Neighbours responded but found nothing to explain the mysterious gas. The police, after a search, were unable to locate the source of the smell.

Mr. Kearney arrived home at about 0030 hours and spotted a stranger at one of the home's windows who was "tall, dressed in dark clothing and wearing a tight-fitting cap". The home-owner chased the stranger but was unable to catch the person.

The press got wind of these incidents, and their sensational handling of the events caused some to claim that they had invented the Mad Gasser themselves. By 5 September there had been four more reports to the police.

After an aborted attack on the Cordes family and further attacks, the panic grew, and people in the city began to arm themselves. The police desperately proposed theories, trying to calm the populace.

The Gasser later hit the Driskell residence, where eleven-year-old Romona was awakened by the sound of someone trying to "remove the storm sash from the window". When the family went to pursue the intruder, Romona was overcome by "fumes" and vomited as her mother spotted a man running away.

On the same night, at about 0145 hours, the Gasser reportedly sprayed his mixture into a room containing several sleeping people, with no noted effect. It is the testimony of Miss Frances Smith, principal of a local school, and her sister Maxine that interests us:

> The first infiltration of gas caught them in their beds. Gasping and choking they awoke and soon felt partial paralysis grip their legs and arms. Later, while awake, the other attacks came and they saw a thin, blue, smoke-like vapor spreading throughout the room. Just before the gas with its flower-like odor came pouring into the room they heard a strange "buzzing" sound outside the house and expressed the belief that the sound was made by the "madman's spraying apparatus" in operation.

After this sighting of the gas itself – that, "thin, blue, smoke-like" vapour – the panic began to die down, and the Mad Gasser disappeared into the annals of Forteana.

One can imagine that, in 1944, as the war still raged overseas, having a prowler running about using gas on citizens would be enough to evoke a panic, and given the reported effects of this gas and its stench, one could hardly blame the residents of Mattoon. The question is, What was this individual using to induce paralysis in the victims?

The Nazis had developed a gas called Tabun by this time, but the symptoms – vomiting, dyspnea, pupillary dilation, hypersalivation, diaphoresis, diarrhea and death – do not match the much milder effects of the gas used in Mattoon, which did sometimes cause vomiting but mostly seemed to cause partial paralysis along with localized burning after exposure.

Was this simply a case of a mad chemist experimenting on innocents or something more paranormal and sinister? We have certainly seen instances of our mysterious mists, especially in relation to UFOs, causing paralysis and other physical effects.

A Portent of Doom?

In *The Brimstone Deceit*, Joshua Cutchin tells a brief story in his discussion of sulphurous smells associated with high strangeness that relates to our topic.

Sulfur's smell can even function as a warning of impending damnation – in the 16th century case of Mistress Kingesfielde, the London housewife proclaimed herself doomed one morning in church after "a smoke or mist came before her eyes with an extreme air of brimstone in her nose".

Now, I can't speak to the good woman's spiritual state, but this seems to me a very good example of a spontaneous episode of what the Celts often called the Sight, or clairvoyance.

I would be most interested in knowing what happened to Mistress Kingesfielde in the days following this vision of smoke and scent of sulfur. Psychic events can be much like dreams, laden with symbolism, and that symbolism tends to be designed to get our attention, sometimes forcefully. I suspect that the mistress was being warned to watch out for accidents or other potentially fatal events in that hazardous time in a way that would clearly get her attention.

Equally, this could have been a warning of some greater disaster about to overtake the community such as a disease outbreak – common in that time.

~

Enlightenment

In the same way that the Sight may produce something ghastly to warn us of potentially catastrophic events, it is also true that visions coincide with mystical experiences. John Mack in his book on abductions gives us this account of a literal enlightenment experience:

> [Dr. Buche] and two friends had spent the evening reading Wordsworth, Keats, Browning and especially Whitman. He was in a state of almost passive enjoyment. All at once, without warning of any kind, he found himself wrapped around, as it were, by a flame-colored cloud ... The next he knew, the light was within himself. Directly afterwards came upon him a sense of exaltation, of immense joyousness accompanied or

> followed by intellectual illumination impossible to describe ...

We have seen more than our fair share of illuminated clouds in this text. Fortunately for the good doctor, this experience seems to have been internal and not one of the clouds that we have seen bear people off to parts unknown or conceal a UFO or cryptid.

A Baby Mammoth?

Speaking of cryptids, in *Monster Diary*, Nick Redfern gives us the smoke story of Jill. This woman enjoyed taking photos of mountains, and Alaska's Mount St. Elias was a "catch" that she wanted for her collection. She was setting up to take a "great shot" when she heard a "funny crunching and thudding on the ground". Jill turned her head in the direction of the sound and was "totally freaked" to see a small mammoth! The creature was about four feet high and raced past her at a good clip, seeming to note her presence and then vanishing in a "small, black cloud of smoke that sucked into itself and was gone".

Mount St. Elias is about 18,009 feet tall, but the witness was at the base of the mountain, not the peak, so altitude was likely not a cause of this sighting. We've already encountered high strangeness around black clouds in this volume and incidences of time slips where the witness lost time. What we have not seen is a cloud that swallowed up a phenomenon from another time.

Mammoths have been extinct for about ten thousand years. I might actually think that there was a relict population of the beasts and that Jill had spotted one in Alaska if it weren't for the bizarre end to the tale. It certainly sounds as though the creature Jill saw had physical presence, what with the crunching and thudding that accompanied the sighting, so we must wonder if this was not either an extraordinarily vivid vision or hallucination or if Jill actually watched a mammoth return to its home time.

~

Scared to Death?

Phantoms and Monsters posted a story on 25 August 2015 that took place in 1889. In this tale, a coroner is puzzled about what caused the death of a young woman.

Ann Georgina Hanks, eighteen, died suddenly in September of 1889, and the circumstances of her death were such that a coroner's inquest was called. During the inquest, the sister of Ms. Hanks' boyfriend, Mary Ann Robinson Maxstead, testified that she accompanied the young woman upstairs to fetch an apron from her bedroom. The deceased was carrying a paraffin lamp.

For some reason, not made clear in the testimony, Ms. Hanks ran her hand around the box where the apron was contained and was startled when "white thick smoke came up about six inches". Ms. Maxstead testified that there was no noise or smell when she saw the smoke.

The deceased collapsed, and the smoke left her hand and dispersed in front of the witness. Ms. Maxstead called for her brother as Ms. Hanks began to scream. The screaming did not stop for half an hour, and the deceased never spoke again or regained consciousness, dying later in the evening.

The next morning, Ms. Maxstead told her brother about the smoke and the "light sparks" that she had seen within it. The coroner's officer and a second witness searched the box for anything that would have caused the smoke. The coroner, Dr.

Hartt, found that the deceased had died of "syncope, following an epileptic fit" and noted that the screaming could have been caused by epilepsy.

The mystery in this case is the smoke. The coroner basically asked Ms. Maxstead, during the inquest, where she came up with this idea, and the young lady "could not say". It sounds to me a lot like the doctor was discomfited by the mystery of this death and was trying to fob the smoke sighting off on a popular diagnosis in those days: female hysteria.

Fainting (syncope) is not a cause of death unless it is related to health issues not noted in the coroner's statements, and fear does not cause epileptic seizures (as the doctor implies), but it can certainly contribute to them. We don't know if the young woman had previously experienced seizures, but the incident itself lasted over thirty minutes. A prolonged seizure, if that is what this was, can kill, so it may be that this suddenly appearing smoke literally frightened this poor woman to death.

While I am willing to accept that this death was the unfortunate result of a seizure, we still have the mystery of the smoke. What was it that Ms. Hanks encountered on or around that box that gave her such a start that it triggered the electrical cascade in her brain that led to her death?

Spontaneous Human Combustion

While we are on the topic of unexplained deaths, one of the strangest causes of death in high strangeness is known as spontaneous human combustion (SHC). In most of these incidents, a person's body is found reduced to nothing but ash and a few bone fragments. The strangeness to these cases is that often, despite the intense heat needed to completely cremate a human body (a cremation retort runs at approximately 1,800 degrees

Fahrenheit), there is very little damage to furniture, walls and other accoutrements surrounding the victim.

Obviously, since the victim is most often alone, which is peculiar in itself, witnesses to such an immolation are rare. Jerome Clark and Nancy Pear did discover one individual who may have had the makings for an SHC, however.

Peter Jones, a California resident, actually saw smoke begin to waft from his body on two separate occasions. The first time, Jones was alone, driving his car, when smoke began to drift from his forearm. Later on, he had smoke whipping out of his feet as he tried to put slippers on. His wife saw the second incident and asked him if he were smoking cigarettes. He was not.

SHC is a rare phenomenon, but it is one that has been documented a number of times in history. If I were Mr. Jones, I would be sleeping with a fire extinguisher near to hand. No one knows the cause of SHC victims' fiery demise, but one would imagine that their experience, like Mr. Jones', began with smoke and then developed into the all-consuming fire that is attested to in the literature.

CONCLUSION

Beginning Thoughts

Even my hometown of San Antonio, Texas, has a curious paranormal smoke story related to the iconic Alamo, an old mission where defenders held off a vastly superior Mexican force during the War of Texas Independence. Their attempt was ultimately unsuccessful but delayed the Mexican army long enough for the Texans to rally and, later, win the war.

Researcher Philip Imbrogno details a story told by tour guides at the Alamo in his book *Haunted Files from the Edge.*

Shortly after the fall of the Alamo and the massacre of its defenders, Santa Anna, the victorious general, ordered one of his subordinate generals to destroy the mission so that it would not be used as a fort again. The general assigned the task to Colonel Sanchez, who took forty men and pulled down the still-standing walls and barriers of the mission compound, leaving only the chapel.

Sanchez was supposedly a religious fellow and had misgivings about tearing down the chapel. Nevertheless, orders were orders, so he commanded his men to take the building down. The demolition did not happen. According to the legend:

As the detail of men approached the walls with picks and hammers to fulfill their orders, they froze in fear as six ghostly entities materialized from the walls of the chapel. The soldiers watched in horror as the "demons" slowly floated toward them waving flaming swords over their heads, while all the time issuing a warning: "Do not touch the walls of this sacred place". Colonel Sanchez and his men dropped their tools and ran away screaming, never to return.

Not to be daunted by mere apparitions, the general who had passed the assignment to the colonel returned to the Alamo with a detachment of men and a cannon. The general, determined to carry out his orders from Santa Anna, ordered his gunners to fire on the chapel and destroy it.

Before this order could be carried out, the "ghostly monks" with fiery swords reappeared. The general, who was a-horse, was unceremoniously dumped from the saddle by his panicked equine.

The commander, apparently, was not very bright. Once more, he gave the order for his gunners to fire on the chapel. Nothing happened. Looking toward the line, he saw his soldiers running for their lives as a wall of fire sprang up around the walls of the mission chapel. The smoke from these flames coalesced into the shape of a "large, imposing man" who then began to throw fireballs at the general.

Finally developing some wisdom, the general fled and reported to Santa Anna, who, after hearing the story, ordered that the chapel not be touched.

Now, remember that this story is legendary, but I found it interesting that the Mexicans saw the ghostly monks and the giant as demons, Imbrogno tries to make the giant man out to be a djinni, and my own first impression, as a Texan who grew up on stories of the valiant defenders of the Alamo (and is named after one), was that this might be an angelic intervention. This difference in perspectives is a great example of the caution we must have in viewing any phenomenon as "evil". We humans are wont to view such episodes through the lens of our own experience and what we think we know.

These kinds of stray stories made researching this book a real pleasure. I have always had a passion for the paranormal, and working my way through the sources in this book was a treat that only a true paranormal geek could enjoy. As you will see from looking at the extensive bibliography for this text, I used sources from history as well as writers that you will probably recognize if you, too, have an interest in these subjects.

After trekking through all these stories, wending my way through cryptid tales, then moving into more spiritual or mostly non-corporeal beings, then jumping into the UFO world before finishing off with mysterious mists and their effects, I found myself in the usual quandary of the paranormal researcher. I wanted answers, but the answers seemed as varied as the phenomena that I examined. Some of the fogs and mists in this book could be explained by completely natural effects, while others seemed so strange that there could be no scientific explanation for them.

I don't think that there is any universal field theory of the paranormal, but I do think that there is a particular sector of human experience that has been largely ignored in the search for a cogent and workable theory of at least some of these mysteries. I am going to outline my thoughts a little later in the conclusion, but, first, I want to look at the natural causes for fog and mist.

~

Natural Causes and the Skeptic's Triad

Looking back over the course of this text, there are some circumstances where a simple mist, fog or other natural phenomenon will really explain the incident. Certainly, there are cases above where the fog seems to be more or less natural, such as the surfer's pterosaurs early in the book or the McCleary sea monster episode, but a fog arising from cool water touching warm air cannot explain people being teleported over long distances or disappearing from the face of the earth.

In those cases where the fog does appear to be natural, let's look at what causes these visual obscurations.

Looking at the website *HowStuffWorks*, I discovered that mist and fog are gradations of the same weather phenomenon: fog. There are actually two common types of fog.

The basic scientific process that creates foggy conditions is called condensation. Basically, this is the process whereby gases turn into liquids, and it describes an action where gas molecules, for whatever reason, lose energy and vibrate less slowly. The gas molecules then have the opportunity to bind together and form a liquid.

Most people, when they think of condensation, think of the process in terms of water vapour. For instance, fogs (and mists) have two well-known processes by which they can be created.

Advection fog is one of the more familiar varieties of this weather phenomenon. Advection fog arises when warm, moist air passes over a cooler surface. The cool surface chills the warm air, and small droplets of water begin to form around latent dust in the atmosphere. These droplets remain airborne and reflect light in all directions, thus impairing visibility.

Mark Mancini, the author of the referenced *HowStuffWorks* article, uses the example of the 1988 Eagles v. Bears playoff game, which became known as the Fog Bowl for the poor visibility during the game, as a good example of advection fog. In that case, warm, humid air from Lake Michigan blew over the much colder air at the stadium and created terrible viewing conditions for the game.

The other usual type of fog is called radiation fog and is most commonly found in valleys or around quiet bodies of water at night. This type of fog is caused by heat, stored in the ground during the day, radiating into the cool air at night.

So what's the difference between fog and mist? Visibility. If you are on flat ground and can see an object on the same horizontal plane at a distance of one kilometre (.62 miles) then you are looking at mist. If that object is obscured, then the phenomenon is considered fog.

Now, while a fog or mist can lend a creepy atmosphere to a scene, as witnessed in countless horror movies, there is nothing in these phenomena that would cause an issue worse than getting lost in the gloom.

We saw, in several of our stories, mists that were illuminated. UFO skeptics have long used the vaunted swamp gas theory to "debunk" any sighting of a light near a swamp or marsh, so I wanted to take a moment to examine what, exactly, swamp gas and swamp lights are.

In an article for *Popular Science*, Benji Jones starts off by relating the well-known occurrence of a traveller spotting a light in a swamp and, thinking it is a candle in the window of a far-off home, making for the light. Of course, the light is not a candle, and the traveller becomes lost in a swamp, sometimes to their doom.

What this traveller has most likely seen is sometimes called ignis fatuus, Latin for foolish fire, a very real phenomenon that produces a ball of flame that can hover for several minutes over a marsh's surface before vanishing into the night. These balls of flame are said to be caused by a "blend of natural gases [rising] to the surface of the mire". The flammable gas that is the culprit for these swamp lights is methane.

The question then arises, what causes the gas burbling from the swamp to ignite and cause the ignis fatuus?

That query is still something of a mystery, but the leading contender for the ignition source is phosphine gas, another by-product of rotting organic matter and one that spontaneously combusts. The theory is that phosphine gas in marshes ignites and causes a burn in the methane produced by all that decaying matter.

Regardless of how these swamp lights occur, they are proven fact, and one can imagine that a swamp light in combination with fog or mist might give someone in the swamp pause. Illuminated mist, anyone? This combination of factors could explain a tiny portion of illuminated mist stories, but, again, these occurrences do not explain the plethora of effects we have seen in the more mysterious mist cases, nor does ignis fatuus explain the perception of structured vehicles as the light source in some mists.

In many ways the use of swamp gas or even ball lightning (a phenomenon that has not yet been scientifically proven) to explain away illuminated mists is yet another example of so-call skeptics grasping at straws to try to debunk the paranormal. You will note my use of the term "so-called skeptic". The dictionary definition of the word skeptic is someone who approaches a problem without preconceived notions. Scientists and others who come at the paranormal with their notion of scientific materialism are not true skeptics but are simply people trying to explain away phenomena that make them uncomfortable.

Additionally, these debunkers will, of course, bring up the tried-and-true skeptic's triad when seeking to discount the occurrences documented in this book and many others. The so-call skeptic will claim that witnesses were mistaken about what they experienced, that they were suffering from hallucinations, or that they are outright lying.

While it is certainly true that some of the witnesses in this book could have assigned paranormal trappings to an incident that they simply perceived as "creepy", I don't think, given the plethora of episodes over a range of paranormal phenomena outlined above, that we can effectively make this argument. A certain small percent of people are going to get excited and report something that wasn't there, but that does not mean that we toss all witness testimony out with the trash. Witness testimony is not flawless, but neither can it be discarded simply because some "skeptic" wants to ignore anecdotal evidence.

I talked extensively about the hallucination/delusion theory in *Phantom Black Dogs: Walkers of the Liminal Way*, so I am not going to repeat myself here. Suffice to say that, again, it may be true that a certain percentage of people were experiencing hallucinations during these incidents, but the stranger accounts that we have on record put the lie to this theory. A hallucination does not cause a person to vanish, for instance, and trying to explain these events as hallucinations begs the question of why, of all the memories and images stored in a human mind, the person would hallucinate something paranormal.

Hoaxes are an ongoing problem in the paranormal world, and they become more complicated with each passing year as computer technology makes it possible to seemingly document things that did not really occur. This fact, added to the willingness of some people to simply lie, for whatever reason, is something that we have to factor into all of our calculations in examining testimony. Still, as you can see throughout the text, the sheer volume of stories gives the lie to the idea that all of the witnesses, or even a significant number of witnesses, are hoaxing.

It seems to me that, while we can assign a small percentage of cases to natural causes and the skeptic's triad, we are still faced with an awful lot of accounts that are mysteries and should be examined more deeply. Like Jenny Randles, the chronicler of the Oz Effect, I believe that something extraordinary is happening in many of these cases where we see effects like a mysterious mist, a feeling of something about to happen, a sudden onset of silence, seeming distortion of time, partial or complete paralysis, and emotional lability.

Randles posits that the Oz Effect may be caused by the presence of UFOs or by what she calls time storms, a seeming displacement in the space-time continuum of unknown origin. Other paranormalists have noted that some factors of the Oz Effect may be seen in the presence of other paranormal entities such as Sasquatch. For my own theory of what might be happening in some of these instances, I am going to detour into a place where many researchers fear to tread.

Magic in the Mist

Whether we like it or not, humankind has a long tradition of shamanism, magic and witchcraft that continues to this day. One of the blind spots that I see in the modern paranormal community (and here I include all the seekers after high strangeness – not just ghosts and spirits) is an almost unreasoning inability to look at these traditions and see what we may learn from them. I suspect that this blind spot has something to do with the effective job that the Abrahamic religions have done in demonizing magical practitioners, but that demonization does not make these people and their very interesting perspective go away.

To be fair, I am seeing a slow change in that attitude, but it is a very slow process and one that I hope will accelerate over the coming years.

To begin our perusal of magical ways of thinking, let's remember the words of the Ho-Chunk elders that Linda Godfrey spoke with in her research on the Sasquatch creatures of her study area:

> Bigfoot is part physical and part spirit, although extremely strong and as "real" as any natural human or animal when in physical form.
>
> They also believe, however, according to Pam's friend, that a Bigfoot can retreat to its spirit form, which may manifest as a light phenomenon, an invisible force, a dense mist or a changing shape of shadow and light, and that in this form it can pop back to its own nonphysical world by accessing certain places that act as openings between this world and the spirit realm. Freshwater springs and ancient, sacred places such as burial mounds or intersections of paths between sacred areas are examples of such places. These openings sound very much like what we would call portals. As for the "alternate" Bigfoot manifestations, we'll discuss all of those forms later in greater detail in relation to contemporary sighting reports.

People who live steeped in an animistic culture, in which everything is alive and potentially has a spirit within, are very likely to agree with at least some of the above, but let's look at the thoughts of others who were concerned with or who practice magic. What we, as paranormalists, need to know is that mysterious mists, fogs, and clouds have been associated with magical practice for centuries.

Reginald Scot, writing in *The Discoverie of Witchcraft* in 1584, describes the calling of a spirit that he calls Balkin. While the description of what happens in this evocation seems to represent a vision state wherein sundry entities appear to the magician, it is interesting to note that, when Balkin and his attendants do finally appear:

> As soon as they come near the Circle, they will breathe out of their mouths a mist, or fog, which will even obscure the light of the Moon, and darken the Magician, that he cannot behold them nor himself; yet let him not be discomfited, or afraid, for that fog will be quickly over ...

At this point, the magician takes up his sword and censer – magical tools used for a specific purpose in the ritual circle – and begins the "form of obligation or binding" upon the spirit, bringing it into his service.

Now, I am not in favour of such coercive techniques in dealing with any living being, spirit or otherwise, but I include this as an early example of mist and smoke being associated with a magical act – that is, the calling forth of a spirit from its Otherworld home. It's also notable that smoke from a censer is an important part of this rite, and in fact, it is said that certain incenses help bring a spirit to manifestation.

I will leave it to the reader to research this topic of incenses. Please be aware that such rituals require intensive training and mental discipline in order to be effective and are not to be undertaken lightly.

In an even earlier witch-hunting manual, the *Malleus Maleficarum*, the author Heinrich Kraemer gives a very graphic method for finding a witch who is alleged to have killed an animal via magic – a common accusation levelled against practitioners in those days. The animal's intestines were to be dragged in a certain manner into the house and then placed over a fire in the kitchen. Such treatment would cause the witch who killed the animal terrific intestinal pain, a good example of what is called sympathetic magic. Note that the witches in this book are almost always female, though men were not excluded from the witch trials.

The witch finders are cautioned to be certain the home is secure before using this method of detection, as the witch will then try to enter the building by any means at her disposal. If she can remove a coal from that fire, her torture will stop.

Further, "when she is unable to enter ... she surrounds [the house] inside and out with the densest fog, with such horrible shrieks and commotions that at last all those in the house think the roof's verily going to fall down ..."

We also see this ability of the witch to project smoke in the Latin text, published in 1680, of *Demoniality* written by a Franciscan priest. This fellow seems to feel that witches and wizards, his term for a male magical practitioner, were busy having sex with the devil to gain their powers. In the priest's view, torture was allowable to coerce a confession from these magic users, especially if, shortly after the act, the person (usually, again, a woman) begins to issue forth black smoke and then levitates. Interestingly, the other sign that a person is a witch is their sudden disappearance after successful conclusion of congress with the devil.

It should be noted here that most of the material in the witch-hunting manuals and the confessions given to witch-finders under torture are the pure fantasy of the sexually repressed minds of the inquisitors. Nevertheless, we have to acknowledge that some of these fantasies may be hung on a bare framework of the experiences of witches and cunning people throughout the ages. The tales of the common folk, who used witches for a variety of purposes, were then twisted into an instrument used against anyone, especially a woman, who did not fit the societal mold or who had land that someone else wanted badly enough to kill for it.

In more modern and, hopefully, enlightened times, noted psychic and magical practitioner Michelle Belanger describes a set of magical workings in their book *Psychic Dreamwalking* that include the construction of a "dream haven", a place from whence the magician may "walk" into the dreamtime and contact other dreamers. Belanger says of this psychic construct that:

> Your dream haven should not be immense. Rather, focus on a space no more than twenty feet in diameter. This is about the size of a large room. This is a manageable size, small enough so you can control each detail, but not so small that you will feel cramped. If you have decided on an outdoor landscape, be sure to define the limits of this space. A sunny hillside does not have walls like a room, but there can be a wall of trees ringing it around, defining the space. Alternately, you can have the space simply fade away after a certain point, so that your dream haven is ringed with mist ...

The dream haven should be equipped with a dream gate, the actual psychic door through which one walks to travel in dreams. Belanger describes their own dream gate as "a huge portal, edged in ivory and horn. Stretched between the pillars of ivory and horn is a surface of swirling mist".

Belanger says that, when they focus on someone, the mist in the dream portal clears, and they can then see that person and step through to them. This writer says that normally the dream walker will appear in the other's dreams, but in one case, someone they attempted to contact in this arcane way, who was not sleeping at the time, saw an apparition of Belanger in his home.

On another psychic tack, many moons ago, I knew a gentleman who practiced the art of scrying. The reader might be familiar with the stereotypical gypsy who looks into a crystal ball as a way of unlocking clairvoyant psychic ability. This fellow used a small, thumb-sized crystal for his scrying surface, and though he got mixed results with the technique, and so did not favour it, told me that, when it worked, he would see mist forming and swirling in the crystal. If he did not stare too intently, but allowed his gaze to remain relaxed, the mist would clear, as in the above account of the dream portal, and he would be able to see some distant event or even future events.

The use of crystal balls and other surfaces is discussed in some detail by Thomas Northcote Whitridge in his book *Crystal Gazing*. In his descriptions of the practice, when the scrying surface triggers a psychic reaction, the surface grows "milky" before clearing and revealing scenes.

Robin Artisson, a modern proponent of traditional witchcraft (as opposed to Wicca), makes reference to the faery, whom he sees as, amongst other things, human ancestors, as the "people of the mist" and, accordingly, relates mist to the land of the dead:

> This is why, in my most recent writing on the Compass [a four directional method of working], I talk about the cycle of the soul, and the mysterious "western direction" – the misty, strange, surreal place that leads away from life, towards the unknown. This is the "Sundown Road" taken by all the world's dead, but that's just poetry; it's referring to the fact that death is a movement towards the strangest and most unknown of places, at least from the perspective of most

> people. In the mist, anything can be concealed, and perhaps it is nothing like anyone can imagine ... I can always speak in generalities, as I have done; I have my own beliefs about certain aspects of the Unseen, and the state or condition of the dead, but there's so much more that I don't know, that what I think could be proven inaccurate in many ways, when I make it across those ancient and mist-choked waters separating Seen from Unseen.

Finally, speaking of the faery, we must check in with noted faery seer Orion Foxwood. Foxwood tells us, in *The Tree of Enchantment*, of something that we have already encountered in the folklore above – the green mist. This seer says that in order to open the way to the faery realms in vision, one must open certain hidden paths and then raise the "Green Mist of Eternal Spring". He even tells us that the opening of the way that he teaches in the book "thins" a space so that "you loosen the grip of your outer senses ... and allow the powers of enchantment and otherworldliness to flow into the area of the working".

Once this opening and other actions are performed, one may journey in vision to the Otherworld. One of the journeys that he portrays is "beneath the ocean or over a body of water to an island. This can be imaged by walking into an ocean that brings you into the otherworld or across a bridge of mist that unfurls from the centre of the room ..."

This is one of many methods for moving through the Otherworld described in the book, but I found it interesting that Foxwood, Artisson and Belanger all use mist as a method of transport. I have done this in a guided meditation practice where, in order to get a person from one place to another in vision, I have encouraged them to walk into a fog bank and then emerge in the other place.

Given this presence of mist as a medium of transport in vision, let's go a little farther with this idea.

To understand this next bit, the reader needs to know a bit about how magicians view their world. As do all people, the magician understands that there is a consensual reality that seems to us to be solid and can be perceived by the five senses. Most people, in their thinking, stop at this "physical" world and never contemplate what physics tells us about the seemingly solid matter that we perceive. Matter is an illusion, but it is a convenient one that we all maintain so that we may function in our world.

Magicians, however, are convinced, from the learning of their tradition and, eventually, personal experience that there is far more to the world than most humans understand. To make this comprehensible, the magic user tends to explain the Other in terms of layers. Each magical system has its own organization to the layers beyond physicality, but I will briefly mention one of the more succinct ones that comes from Jason Miller's fascinating work, *The Sorcerer's Secret*.

Miller notes, at the outset of his presentation "that some of these systems [of detailing the movement of energy from the physical to the more subtle realms] entail dozens of layers and sub-layers giving quite detailed descriptions of the role and potential of each". Miller then goes on to say that "for our purposes, we can rely upon a simple three level system, such as the one presented in the Chaldean Oracles".

The first level is the material world in which we exist:

> It contains within it three levels of its own: non-living, living, and etheric substance. Non-living substance is not only matter that we see around us such as concrete and such, but electricity and magnetism and other energies that can be measured with scientific instruments. Living substance

> counts not only as flesh and bone, but bio-energy. **Etheric substance acts as a bridge between [the other levels and the material level**] [emphasis mine].

The next level Miller calls the Aetherial Realm. "It is the world of the subtle elements of pure fire, water, air, and earth". At the lowest end of the level exist an innumerable population of spirits and the subtle energy that some cultures call chi, ki, prana, lung, odic force, etc. This is also the place of the astral body, and, in its higher levels, it is the home of Archetypes, Angels, the Intelligences of Planets as well as gods and goddesses of myth.

Finally, we come to the Empyrean, Akashic or Divine Realm. "The gods here exist in their highest and most cosmic transcendent nature. There is no hint at this level of the classic mythology that tells of fights and affairs between gods ... we are beyond all that and dealing with cosmic and causal forces".

While the level system is very interesting, for our purposes, it is Miller's statement that etheric substance is a bridge between the other levels and our own plane that is most important. I will return to this idea in the next section of this conclusion.

Now that I have drawn some correlation between mists and magical practice, let's move on to some thoughts about how this relates to our subject and the mysteries that we have seen in the mist.

~

What's Magic Got To Do With It?

Let's perform a thought exercise. In this exercise, the forces of religion and scientific materialism never gained a stranglehold on Western education, and in the course of the lessons, children and university students learned about the history of magic and some of its observations about our world. Students would learn, for example, that Sir Isaac Newton, recognized as a scientific pioneer, was obsessed with alchemy, the mystical precursor to our modern chemistry. The young would also learn that scientific, double-blind, random studies – the gold standard of the scientific method – have repeatedly shown the existence of such phenomena as telepathy and other psi events.

Instead of viewing magic with a gimlet eye, our learners would be taught to view the working of magic with an open mind. Most students would probably roll their eyes, as they do at learning history or Shakespeare, and go home to play video games, but those who were intrigued would have access to sources, tools and teachers that would allow them to explore more deeply.

If those same students happened to have an interest in the paranormal, then their exploration of magic would yield gold for them because magic provides a perfectly legitimate framework for how the inner planes work and how those inner planes relate to our world. This structure ties in with the three levels of being that we talked about in the earlier magic section.

As we discussed, there are innumerable spirits living in the plane that is "closest" to ours (these planes could more accurately be said to overlap, but the idea of layers is easier to grasp). In magic, there is a process called evocation, which, as I have mentioned, is the process of calling to a spirit in the Aetherial realm and asking it to make its presence known here on the Material plane. As I have also mentioned previously, these presences do not typically assume any sort of physical form but may be visible to the human eye under certain circumstances.

As a side note, the idea amongst some paranormalists that all paranormal phenomena are caused by a certain type of spirit (djinn or demons being popular with some) is simply incorrect according to magical thinking. Even looking at one of Katharine Brigg's encyclopedic works on the faery will give the reader some idea of the vast sweep of spirits that have been identified under the faery classification. This classification does not consider beings like angels, demons, elementals, the human dead, and other spirits that cannot be so easily classified.

The process of evocation, at its roots, involves knowing what spirit you are looking for (preferably by name) and having developed the authority to call that spirit, usually by having contact with one's highest self (a process that requires considerable training in meditation and visualization, in and of itself). A successful evocation has certain elements that we should, by now, recognize.

Practitioners that I have known report that as they set up for the calling and then as they send the call forth, it seems as though sound around them is muted, and their time sense becomes distorted. Depending on the type of spirit being summoned, there is a feeling of presentiment before the spirit appears and physical sensations such as the electrostatic feel noted in some of our cases. There are also reports of odd sounds, including human speech (though often in a language the practitioner does not understand), movement of objects in the vicinity of the magical enclosure, and the formation of a spirit body in the smoke of incense used in the rite.

These effects may certainly be personal to the mage and the result of enhanced psychic vision brought about by the rite of evocation. Nevertheless, we can't help but note some similarities between these effects, noted by magicians in the modern era, and the high strangeness that surrounds our mist tales.

Remember, too, that these effects come to pass as the result of a human working at communication beyond the veil that separates the Material from the Aetherial. There is no expectation that a physical being is going to manifest as the result of the working, only that the spirit will be contacted and requested to assist the mage.

Interestingly, though, there are mages who believe that some of the residents of the Aetherial plane can make the transition from their plane to our own by their own power and for their own purposes. Remember Jason Miller's statement about the etheric energies of the Material plane providing a bridge between the other planes and ours? Some mages feel that this idea is not only true but that those etheric energies provide the spirit coming through from another plane with a means for clothing itself in solid form.

The classic example of this concept is an angel. A resident of the Aetherial plane, an angel is a powerful messenger spirit whose purpose requires that it sometimes interacts physically with the Material world. When required to do so by its mission, the angel "descends" from the Aetherial, takes etheric substance from the "upper" material plane, and assumes what appears to be a physical body. Once it has completed its mission, the angel then reverses this process and seemingly vanishes from sight. The being has not gone away. It has simply returned to its more natural form on the Aetherial plane.

If angels can do this, then it follows that other spirits can as well. I would love to see someone get a good DNA sample from a Sasquatch and identify the creatures as a new ape species or relict hominid. However, there are far too many Sasquatch stories where the creature is seen to vanish, its footprints disappear, or only one footprint is found, for us to ignore the possibility that Sasquatch might be something more than an unknown animal. It's possible that the Hairy Man is a species of spirit that can do this trick of taking on form and then leaving it behind just as the Ho-Chunk conjecture. This theory would certainly explain the high strangeness associated with Sasquatch.

So why, you might ask, does it seem that there are hot spots or window areas or portals or whatever you want to call them around the world? Again, our students of magic and psychism would be able to supply some thoughts in this regard.

I am writing these words on Halloween, more traditionally called Samhain (pronounced approximately sow-en) amongst modern Neo-pagans. This time period is regarded as a time when the Veil Between the Worlds is thinnest and, for pagans, is a time of associating with the ancestors and/or placating the fae resident to their area.

If there are times during the year when the Veil is thin, then it makes sense that beings wanting to visit our plane might use those times to ease their transition.

It's also true that certain places on the Earth's surface, such as the stone circles of Europe or the Medicine Wheels of the indigenous people of North America as well as natural formations like the Hockomock Swamp in Massachusetts are seen as places where the spirit world more closely approaches our own Material plane. Again, it makes sense spirits would use the thinness of the Veil in those locations to ease their transit onto our plane and thus give these areas a reputation as "window areas". There is a whole school of geomantic magic that offers more explanation about why these spots are "thin" but suffice to say that the theory of ley lines, which I discussed briefly in my previous work, has considerable bearing on this theory.

Finally, I noted in my book on Phantom Black Dogs that there is an embarrassment of riches when it comes to information on magical practices in this day and age. One has only to walk into a local bookstore or go online to a book retailer to find everything one needs to begin a magical practice. While many people dabble with the occult, discover that it is hard work and then leave it be, others become fascinated by it and follow their passion into one or the other traditions of the mage's art.

These dedicated practitioners have a tendency to favour certain areas for their work – an indoor temple, an outdoor grove, a faery ring in the forest, etc. – and according to the theories of magic, the energy raised and used in these spots eventually has a thinning effect on the Veil in that area. This concept may apply to ancient temples, such as the stone circles and Medicine Wheels mentioned above, as well as ancient burial sites. I think there is a strong magical reason for the correlation between Manwolf sightings and the presence of the so-called burial mounds left by indigenous peoples.

I recall with some fondness reading about the wild things witnessed on the Diné (Navajo) reservation during J. C. Johnson's lifetime and referenced in the *Monsters and Magic* blog. As the writer of that blog points out:

> ... Mr. Johnson and his team operate on a reservation where it is not at all uncommon for people to consult with medicine people for the relief of their illnesses while at the same time availing themselves of Indian Health Services. The Dine' have a complex and beautiful ritual life full of ceremonies to keep them in balance with their land. Those ceremonies make reference to their gods and draw on the power of their myths to bring about this balancing effect. As with all good ceremony, ways are opened to the Otherworld and spirits and energies flow through freely. The singer is taught how to open those ways and how to close them down again but such ceremonies are bound to leave a residue of power on the land.

The writer's point, and my own, is that the land of the Diné is steeped in shamanic traditions and practice and is therefore "thin" in some spots and liable to visits from the Otherworld.

In this case, these incursions seem to have included everything from giant, prehistoric lizard creatures to completely mythical beings such as centaurs. It should be noted that the notorious Skinwalker Ranch is located in land known to the neighbouring Utes as being related to skinwalkers, a type of shaman known for harmful practices in that region.

To conclude, we have seen that the magical practice of evocation can cause effects similar to some of the ones that we saw throughout this book. We have further seen that that magical theory gives us several reasons why the Veil Between the Worlds might be thin at certain times or in some spots. We have also seen that, in these places where the Veil is thin, magical theory tells us that certain spirits can "walk" from their plane into our Material world and gather etheric substance to themselves. This substance gives the spirit physical presence on our plane and the ability to leave footprints and other signs of the incursion.

It is my belief that the fogs, mists, and cloud-like structures that we have been seeing throughout this text are signs of openings between the Material plane and the Aetherial world of innumerable spirits. The mist that develops, along with all the multitudinous effects that we have seen, are an indication that the Veil has been breached. As we've seen from looking at evocation, silence and distortion of time, two of the major things that we see in many of our cases, would naturally occur when such rifts occur.

The strong physical reactions that some people experience when coming into contact with these anomalies could be explained by the theory of resonance. A mage doing an evocation is bringing themselves into resonance with the spirit they are calling. In other words, the rite of evocation, when done properly, causes the mage to vibrate at a frequency that will "mesh" with the frequency of the spirit they are calling.

A civilian caught during such an incursion has no time for preparation (even if they knew what to do) and suffers from coming into contact with energy that is not harmonious with their body. This effect might be described as something like plugging a 120-volt device into a 200-volt socket.

Disappearances and teleportations could be accounted for simply by looking at the stories of those who blundered into faery. Some of those people, like the Rev. Robert Kirk, were never seen again. Others emerged from the faery realm only to discover that long periods of time had passed and all the people they knew were dead. Still others were fortunate enough to escape the faery realm or be ejected from it and often wound up in places other than their home village.

Both space and time seem to work differently in the Otherworld, and the stories of the faery are good indicators of this idea, but they are by no means the only indicators. As I've said earlier in the text, there is a whole body of djinn lore in the Middle East, for example, that tells us much the same thing. Anyone who interacts with the Otherworld, voluntarily or otherwise, is affected by that interaction in a positive or negative way, depending on the nature of the interaction.

Again, I am not attempting a universal field theory of the paranormal in this conclusion. As I've noted, I am a both/and thinker. I present this information, gleaned from decades of personal research, as yet another piece of the puzzle that is the paranormal.

I realize that not all people will be comfortable with the ideas that I have presented above. I do not provide this tour of magical thought so that people will accept it as gospel. I simply want the reader to look at these ideas and think: *Wow, I've never heard of that? I wonder ...*

For, after all, wonder is why we became enthralled with these mysteries in the first place, and wonder is why many a mage and paranormalist has begun their long wander down those winding paths. It is the innate curiosity of human beings that leads us to plunge “down the rabbit hole” looking for answers, and it is our love of mystery that keeps us searching and hoping for answers around the next corner.

BIBLIOGRAPHY

Books and Articles:

- Artisson, Robin. *Letters from the Devil's Forest.* Black Malkin Press, 2014.
- Balzano, Christopher. *Ghostly Adventures: Chilling Stories from America's Haunted Hot Spots.* Fall River Press, 2008.
- Balzano, Christopher. *Picture Yourself Ghost Hunting: Step-by-Step Instruction for Exploring Haunts and Finding Spirits, Spooks, and Specters.* Cengage Learning, 2009.
- Baring-Gould, Sabine. *The Book of Werewolves (originally published 1865).* Senate, 1995.
- Belanger, M. *Psychic Dreamwalking: Explorations at the Edge of Self.* Weiser Books, 2006.
- Blackburn, L. *Lizard Man: The True Story of the Bishopville Monster.* Anomalist Books, 2013.

- Bord, Janet. *Fairies: Real encounters with little people.* Michael O'Mara Books, 2014.
- Briggs, Katharine Mary. *The Vanishing People; a Study of Traditional Fairy Beliefs*. BT Batsford Limited, 1978.
- Bruce, Robert. *The Practical Psychic Self-Defense Handbook: A Survival Guide.* Hampton Roads Publishing, 2011.
- Clark, J. And Pear, N. *Strange and Unexplained Happenings: When Nature Breaks the Rules of Science.* Gale Group, 1995.
- Clark, Jerome. *Unexplained!: Strange Sightings, Incredible Occurrences & Puzzling Physical Phenomena.* Visible Ink Press, 1998.
- Coleman, L. *Curious Encounters: Phantom Trains, Spooky Spots, and Other Mysterious Wonders.* Faber & Faber, 1989.
- Coleman, L. *Mothman: Evil Incarnate.* Cosimo, 2017.
- Coleman, L. *Mysterious America: The Ultimate Guide to the Nation's Weirdest Wonders, Strangest Spots, and Creepiest Creatures.* Gallery Books, 2017.
- Constable, Trevor James. *Sky Creatures: The Newly Revised and Re-edited Edition of the Underground Classic "The Cosmic Pulse of Life"*. Pocket Books, 1978.
- Corliss, William. *Handbook of Unusual Natural Phenomena*. Arlington House, 1986.
- Creighton, Gordon. "Teleportations". *Flying Saucer Review*, 1970.
- Creighton, Gordon. "More on Teleportations". *Flying Saucer Review*, 1970.
- Cutchin, Joshua. *The Brimstone Deceit: An In-Depth Examination of Supernatural Scents, Otherworldly Odors, and Monstrous Miasma.* Anomalist Books, 2016.

- Cutchin, Joshua. *Thieves in the Night: A Brief History of Supernatural Child Abductions*. Anomalist Books, 2018.
- Dash, Mike. *Borderlands: The Ultimate Exploration of the Unknown*. Overlook Press, 2000.
- Edwards, Frank. *Strange World*. Bantam Books, 1969.
- Evans-Wentz, Walter Yeeling. *The Fairy-Faith in Celtic Countries: The Classic Study of Leprechauns, Pixies, and Other Fairy Spirits*. Citadel Press, 2003.
- Foxwood, Orion. *The Tree of Enchantment: Ancient Wisdom and Magic Practices of the Faery Tradition*. Weiser Books, 2008.
- Gerhard, Ken. *Encounters with Flying Humanoids: Mothman, Manbirds, Gargoyles & Other Winged Beasts*. Llewellyn Worldwide, 2013.
- Godfrey, Linda S. *American Monsters: A History of Monster Lore, Legends, and Sightings in America*. Penguin, 2014.
- Godfrey, Linda S. *I Know What I Saw: Modern-Day Encounters with Monsters of New Urban Legend and Ancient Lore*. Penguin, 2019.
- Godfrey, Linda S. *Monsters Among Us: An Exploration of Otherworldly Bigfoots, Wolfmen, Portals, Phantoms, and Odd Phenomena*. Penguin, 2016.
- Godfrey, Linda S. *The Beast of Bray Road: Tailing Wisconsin's Werewolf*. Big Earth Publishing, 2003.
- Godfrey, Linda S. *Werewolves: Mysteries, Legends, and Unexplained Phenomenon*. Chelsea House Publishing, 2008.
- Godfrey, Linda S., et al. *Weird Wisconsin: Your Travel Guide to Wisconsin's Local Legends and Best Kept Secrets*. Sterling Publishing Company, Inc., 2005.

- Greer, J. M. *Monsters: An Investigator's Guide to Magical Beings.* Llewelyn Publications, 2001.
- Guiley, R. E. *The Djinn Connection: The Hidden Links Between Djinn, Shadow People, ETs, Nephilim, Archons, Reptilians and Other Entities.* Visionary Living, Inc., 2013.
- Guiley, R. E. *The Vengeful Djinn: Unveiling the Hidden Agenda of Genies.* Llewellyn Publications, 2011.
- Harpur, Patrick. *Daimonic reality: A field guide to the otherworld.* Viking Arkana, 1994.
- Holzer, Hans. *Ghosts: True Encounters with the World Beyond.* Black Dog & Leventhal Publishers, Incorporated, 2004.
- Imbrogno, P. *Haunted Files from the Edge: A Paranormal Investigator's Explorations into Infamous Legends & Extraordinary Manifestations.* Llewelyn Publications, 2012.
- Jones, Marie D. *Modern Science and the Paranormal.* Rosen Publishing, 2009.
- Keel, John A. *Our Haunted Planet.* Galde Press, Inc., 1999.
- Kelleher, Colm A., and George Knapp. *Hunt for the Skinwalker: Science Confronts the Unexplained at a Remote Ranch in Utah.* Simon and Schuster, 2005.
- Kirtley, Bacil F. "Dracula: The Monastic Chronicles and Slavic Folklore". *Midwest Folklore,* Autumn 1956, Vol. 6, No. 3.
- Krämer, Heinrich. *Malleus Maleficarum.* First Published in 1486–1487, J Rodker, 1928.
- Lebling, Robert. *Legends of the Fire Spirits: Jinn and Genies from Arabia to Zanzibar.* I.B. Tauris, 2010.
- McCue, Peter A. *Britain's Paranormal Forests: Encounters in the Woods.* The History Press, 2019.

- Mack, John. *Abduction: Human Encounters with Aliens*. MacMillan, 1994.
- Michaels, Susan. *Sightings: Beyond Imagination Lies the Truth*. Fireside, 1996.
- Miller, Jason. *The Sorcerer's Secret: Strategies in Practical Magick*. New Page, 2009.
- Murgoci, Agnes. "The Vampire in Roumania". *Folklore,* 31 December 1926, Vol. 37, No.4.
- Nicholson, Andrew. *Weird Australia: Real Reports of Uncanny Creatures*. Self-published, 2017.
- O'Brien, Chris. *Secrets of the Mysterious Valley*. Adventures Unlimited Press, 2007.
- O'Brien, Chris. *Stalking the Herd: Unravelling the Cattle Mutilation Mystery*. Adventures Unlimited Press, 2014.
- Offutt, Jason. *Darkness Walks: The Shadow People Among Us*. Anomalist Books, 2009.
- Perkowski, Jan L. *Vampires of the Slavs*. Slavica Publishers Inc., 1976.
- Pratt, Bob. *UFO Danger Zone: Terror and Death in Brazil – Where Next?* Horus House Press, Inc.,1996.
- Randles, Jenny. *Strange But True?* London Bridge, 1996.
- Randles, Jenny. *Time Storms: Amazing Evidence for Time Warps, Space Rifts and Time Travel*. Piatkus, 2001.
- Redfern, N. *Shapeshifters: Morphing Monsters and Changing Cryptids*. Llewelyn Publications, 2017.
- Redfern, N. *The Real Men in Black: Evidence, Famous Cases, and True Stories of These Mysterious Men and their Connection to the UFO Phenomenon*. New Page, 2011.
- Redfern, N. "The Sounds of Sasquatch". *Wood*

Knocks, Volume 1: Journal of Sasquatch Research. Edited by David Weatherly. Leprechaun Press, 2016.

- Rieti, Barbara. *Strange terrain: the fairy world in Newfoundland*. No. 45. St. John's, Nfld.: Institute of Social and Economic Research, Memorial University of Newfoundland, 1991.
- Scot, Reginald. *The Discoverie of Witchcraft*. Reprint of first edition published in 1584, Elliot Stock, 1186.
- Shuker, Karl. *The Unexplained: An Illustrated Guide to the World's Natural and Paranormal Mysteries*. Barnes & Noble Books, 1997.
- Sinistrari. Rev. Father, of Ameno. *Demoniality or Incubi and Succubi*. English translation with Latin text from 1680, Isidore Lisieux, 1879.
- Spence, Lewis. *The Fairy Tradition in Britain*. Rider, 1948.
- Stead, William Thomas, ed. *Real Ghost Stories: A Record of Authentic Apparitions: Being the Christmas Number of the Review of Reviews*. Publishing Office of the Review of Reviews, 1891.
- Steiger, Brad. *Beyond Belief: Strange, True Mysteries of the Unknown*. Scholastic, 1991.
- Steiger, Brad. *Real Monsters, Gruesome Critters, and Beasts from the Darkside*. Visible Ink Press, 2010.
- Steiger, Brad. *Strange Disappearances*. Lancer Books, 1972.
- Stewart, R.J. *Robert Kirk: Walker Between the Worlds – A new Edition of The Secret Commonwealth of Elves, Fauns, and Fairies*. R J Stewart Books, 2007.
- Strieber, Whitley. *Communion: A True Story*. William Morrow Paperbacks, Reprint Edition, 2008.
- Strieber, Whitley and Kripal, Jeffrey. *The Super*

Natural: Why The Unexplained Is Real. TarcherPerigree, 2017.

- Treat, W. *Weird Texas: Your Travel Guide to Texas's Local Legends and Best Kept Secrets.* Sterling Publishing Co., 2005.
- Turner, Karla. *Taken: Inside the Alien-Human Abduction Agenda*. Keltworks, 1994.
- Vallee, Jacques. *Confrontations: A Scientist's Search for Alien Contact.* Ballantine Books, 1990.
- Vallee, Jacques. *Dimensions: A Casebook of Alien Contact.* Contemporary Books, 1988.
- Vallee, Jacques. *Revelations: Alien Contact and Human Deception.* Ballantine Books, 1991.
- Watson, W. T. *Phantom Black Dogs: Walkers of the Liminal Way*. Beyond the Fray Publishing, 2021.
- Whitridge, Thomas N. *Crystal Gazing: Its History and Practice, with a discussion of the evidence for telepathic scrying.* Alexander Morning Limited: The De La More Press, 1905.
- Winfield, M., Koerner, J., Shaw, T, and Lockhart, R. *Haunted Rochester: A Supernatural History of the Lower Genesee.* The History Press, 2008.

From the Internet

- Admin. "Crypto Four Corners". *Monsters and Magic,* 06 May 2014. https://monstersandmagic.wordpress.com/2014/05/06/crypto-four-corners/
- Admin. "True UFO Encounters". *Unexplained.* Last updated 25 February 2014. https://unexplained.co/paranormal-articles/true-ufo-encounters/3368/
- Editors of Publications International, Ltd. "The Rendlesham Forest Incident". *How Stuff Works*, 21

February 2008. https://science.howstuffworks.com/space/aliens-ufos/rendlesham-forest-incident.htm

- Everts, Sarah. "The Nazi Origins of Deadly Nerve Gases". *Chemical & Engineering News*, 17 October 2016. https://cen.acs.org/articles/94/i41/Nazi-origins-deadly-nerve-gases.html
- Freeman, T. and Treat, W. "Black Mist of Casa Grande Mountain". Weird U.S., unknown date. http://www.weirdus.com/states/arizona/unexplained_phenomena/black_mist_casa_grande_mtn/index.php
- Germer, W., host. "Terror in the Woods". *Sasquatch Chronicles*. Episode 473. 22 September 2018. https://sasquatchchronicles.com/sc-ep473-terror-in-the-woods/
- Harper, Scott. "True Story: Dancing Ghost Cattle?" *Phantoms and Monsters*. 21 January 2015. https://www.phantomsandmonsters.com/2015/01/true-story-dancing-ghost-cattle.html
- Holly, Chris. "The Roommates and the Spaceman of Ocean Beach". *Endless Journey with the Unknown*, 2016. http://endlessjrny.blogspot.com/2016/08/the-roommates-and-spaceman-of-ocean.html
- Jones, B. "The Swamp Science That Lured Travelers to Their Doom – And Inspired the Jack-o'-Lantern". *Popular Science*, 31 October 2018. https://www.popsci.com/jack-o-lanterns-marsh-lights/
- Mancini, M. "Are Mist and Fog The Same?". *HowStuffWorks*, date not cited. https://science.howstuffworks.com/environmental/earth/geophysics/are-fog-and-mist-the-same.htm
- Pittman, C. "The Bridgewater Triangle". *The*

Bridgewater Triangle, 2008. http://www.cellarwalls.com/ufo/btriangle.htm

- Redfern, N. "Freaky Fog, Mysterious Mist, and the World of the Paranormal". *Mysterious Universe*. 17 May 2020. https://mysteriousuniverse.org/2020/05/freaky-fog-mysterious-mist-and-the-world-of-the-paranormal/
- Strickler, L. "Scared to Death". *Phantoms and Monsters*, 25 August 2015. https://www.phantomsandmonsters.com/2015/08/scared-to-death.html
- Strickler, L. "The Big Grey Man of Ben MaćDhui". *Phantoms and Monsters*, 07 May 2014. https://www.phantomsandmonsters.com/2014/05/the-big-grey-man-of-ben-macdhui.html
- Strickler, Lon. "The Imjarvi Contacts". *Phantoms and Monsters*, 21 March 2015. https://www.phantomsandmonsters.com/2015/03/the-imjarvi-contacts.html
- Swancer, Brent. "Vanishings and High Strangeness at Africa's Cursed Mountain". *Mysterious Universe*, 04 January 2017. https://mysteriousuniverse.org/2017/01/vanishings-and-high-strangeness-at-africas-cursed-mountain/
- Vera, A. And Said, S. "A Boy Who Was Lost In the Woods Says a Bear Kept Him Company". *CNN*, 29 January 2019. https://www.cnn.com/2019/01/28/us/casey-hathaway-bear-claims/index.html
- Admin. "Mirror, Mirror". *Monsters and Magic*. 31 May 2016. https://monstersandmagic.wordpress.com/2016/05/31/mirror-mirror/
- Staff Writer. "Mystery Creature Caught On Camera". *Wales Online*. 03 April 2008. https://www.

walesonline.co.uk/news/local-news/mystery-creature-caught-on-camera-2180075

- Wagner, S. "What Was That Unexplained Fog or Smoke?". *Liveaboutdotcom*. 11 December 2018. https://www.liveabout.com/what-was-that-unexplained-fog-smoke-2597188
- Wikipedia. "Mothman". *Wikipedia*. Last edited 11 October 2021. https://en.wikipedia.org/wiki/Mothman
- Wikipedia. "Randy Gardner sleep deprivation experiment". *Wikipedia*. Last edited 28 August 2021. https://en.wikipedia.org/wiki/Randy_Gardner_sleep_deprivation_experiment
- Wikipedia. "Rendlesham Forest Incident". Wikipedia. Last edited 7 September 2021. https://en.wikipedia.org/wiki/Rendlesham_Forest_incident

About the Author

W. T. Watson is a coffee addict with an abiding love of monsters, magic, Forteana and the paranormal that infuses his fictional works. When he is not writing or reading about monsters, he can be found outdoors allowing his dogs to take him for a walk around his neighbourhood in Kitchener, Ontario.

He lives with his spouse, Stacey, in a townhome that would be jammed with books if it weren't for e-readers.

ALSO BY W.T. WATSON

Hunting The Beast: A Novel

Phantom Black Dogs: Walkers of the Liminal Way

www.ingramcontent.com/pod-product-compliance
Lightning Source LLC
Chambersburg PA
CBHW032347280326
41935CB00008B/482

* 9 7 8 1 9 5 4 5 2 8 2 5 3 *